The Reluctant Psychic

The Reluctant Psychic

Richard J West

AuthorHouse™ UK Ltd.
1663 Liberty Drive
Bloomington, IN 47403 USA
www.authorhouse.co.uk
Phone: 0800.197.4150

© 2014 Richard J West. All rights reserved.

No part of this book may be reproduced, stored in a retrieval system, or transmitted by any means without the written permission of the author.

Published by AuthorHouse   03/21/2014

ISBN: 978-1-4918-9630-3 (sc)
ISBN: 978-1-4918-9631-0 (hc)
ISBN: 978-1-4918-9632-7 (e)

Any people depicted in stock imagery provided by Thinkstock are models, and such images are being used for illustrative purposes only.
Certain stock imagery © Thinkstock.

Because of the dynamic nature of the Internet, any web addresses or links contained in this book may have changed since publication and may no longer be valid. The views expressed in this work are solely those of the author and do not necessarily reflect the views of the publisher, and the publisher hereby disclaims any responsibility for them.

To Sally

Thanks for putting up with me and supporting my every move.
It can't be easy!

Acknowledgements

I owe a debt of gratitude to all the wonderful people who have arrived, unbidden, into my life to guide, teach, and support me at the appropriate moment.

It has taken me many years to realize the truth of the old saying, "When the student is ready, the teacher will appear," but it really is the case.

My thanks to Mel Bronstein, who arrived into my life to provide, as he put it, "wake-up time". He was my mentor in the early, difficult days, always appearing on cue when he was needed even when he was on the other side of the Atlantic Ocean.

To my dear friends Keith and Marguerite, who have steadfastly supported, cajoled, and led me into new pastures and experiences over many years. They have opened many doors into a world of which, without them, I could only have dreamed.

Thank you to Nannette, who appeared in my life at the most apposite moment to help me develop and hone my abilities in ways that I never could have imagined possible.

To my family, who watched my transformation without judgement and always supported me, thanks from the bottom of my heart!

And thank you to all of the souls and personalities that I have had the privilege to interact with over the years, from whom I have learnt so much!

He is not lost our dearest love,

Nor has he travelled far.

Just stepped inside home's loveliest room

And left the door ajar.

If only we could see the splendour of the land,

To which our loved ones are called from you and me

We'd understand.

If only we could hear the welcome they receive,

From old familiar voices all so dear

We would not grieve.

If only we could know the reason why they went

We'd smile and wipe away the tears that flow

And wait content.

(Anonymous)

Part One

My Story

I was born in 1947 in Dover, in a little Victorian terraced house which clung to the hillside. It was constantly shaken by trains passing by at the end of the cul-de-sac. The eldest of two siblings, I grew up in a happy and secure environment. My father, Fred, had returned from the war after seven long years in the Burmese jungles, fighting alongside the courageous Gurkhas.

My mother, a sensitive and kind person, had spent the war years in the women's Auxiliary Fire Service in the centre of Hellfire Corner. It was called this because Dover bore the brunt of the long-range artillery that Hitler had placed on the other side of the English Channel to wreak havoc on a daily basis and destroy the morale of the local populace.

My parents described me as a sensitive lad, something that I could never understand. With hindsight, I now see that during my childhood and youth, there were several unusual occurrences that began gently persuading me that there was more to this life than I had ever imagined.

My first memory of such an event was when I was six years old. I was very ill with meningitis. As I lay in my darkened bedroom, unable to bear the daylight, I listened intently for the sound of my friends with whom I usually played in the street outside. However, they had been told that I was seriously ill, so they should make no loud noises.

Outside the closed bedroom door, I heard Doctor Browne, our general practitioner, telling my parents that they should prepare themselves for the worst. No sooner had he uttered those words than my room became diffused with a soft light, and I experienced a feeling of intense love. A voice said, "You will not die. You have work to do." I drifted off into a peaceful sleep, and when I awoke many hours later, I had turned the corner and was well on the road to recovery.

Being so young, I genuinely didn't think that this was anything unusual. When a soft, warm light and feelings of peace and love washed over me, on regular occasions in the future, I felt that I was being looked after as I drifted into a peaceful sleep.

Over the ensuing years, I developed what can only be described as a knowing about people and places. Although it proved to be of great value in later life, it was distinctly unpleasant for an adolescent.

Having returned from the war a hero, my father found it hard to make ends meet—as did many other returning servicemen. He was a skilled mechanic, so he undertook work for the many fishermen in Dover, repairing and maintaining the engines of their fishing boats. During the winter months, these boats were dragged up the shingle beach at East Cliff and into a series of caves and tunnels dug deep into the famous White Cliffs of Dover. Here he could work, staying safe and dry while the winter winds howled outside.

He brought me with him on many occasions to pass him tools as he worked in the cramped confines of the engine housings. I grew to hate these visits and became fearful of the presences I felt there. They seemed to loom out of the darkness of the many tunnels that radiated out from the central cavern. I became convinced that malevolent energies were just waiting to suck the life out of me if I ventured out of the safety of the oil lamp's illumination.

Many years later, I learned the reason for these feelings of fear and despair. I discovered that these caves were hewn out of the soft, white chalk in the early 1750s and were in use as homes for almost a hundred years.

In 1939, the complex of caves and tunnels was used to provide deep shelter for up to 23,550 persons. They were well used, as the town came under constant bombardment in the Second World War. The structure saw much pain and heartache during those difficult times. Many lost souls who perished in terrible circumstances sought shelter from the terrors of the times in the only place that they knew would protect them.

As a teenager, the vicar asked me to serve as an altar boy in St Andrew's, the local twelfth-century church, mainly to avoid my terrible voice from spoiling the choir! It was there that, once again, I experienced the abject terror of being alone in the shadows and half-light. Whenever I was by my self in the vestry, the hairs on my forearms and the back of my neck stood on end, my heart pounded, and my legs turned to jelly. I was filled with a malevolence that I came to know well in my later years as an experienced dowser and ghostbuster, but as a teenager wet behind the ears, I just fled the scene!

In the forthcoming years, I often experienced such sensations, both happy and frightening, and I gradually learnt to trust that what I was feeling was a valid experience.

When my mother was killed in a tragic road accident several years later, I was distraught, heartbroken, and totally lost. A few days after her funeral, which I was prevented from attending, I found myself standing outside the big blue doors of the local Spiritualist church several miles away from my home, wondering how I had gotten there.

This was total anathema to my upbringing, and I was about to leave when I heard a warm and friendly male voice say, "Inside these doors are the answers to all your questions." That was enough to send me fleeing as fast as my legs would carry me, and I resolved never to have anything to do with such goings-on ever again. If only I had known then what my future would hold.

Some while later, I was sitting comfortably in an armchair, staring at a crackling fire as the evening light faded. The room was dim, and I was in a state of warm contentment when my peace was disturbed. The same warm, friendly voice that I had heard outside the church said, "Richard, will you let me in?" I was really frightened, and it hardened my resolve not to get involved in anything psychic in the future.

In 1967 I was lucky enough to be selected to become a preventive officer in the Waterguard division of Her Majesty's Customs and Excise Service. It soon became apparent that my ability was exactly suited to catching smugglers and detecting contraband, and my success rate was far and away above the norm.

I settled happily into my role and enjoyed many years of satisfying adventures until 1972, when the Waterguard, which I had come to love, was disbanded and absorbed into the general tax collecting system. I decided to move on and see what other adventures the world had to offer.

How It All Began

Having married, had two children, and run a successful building and replacement window company, I continued to use my knowing skills to good advantage. Life as a company director was fulfilling and satisfying.

However, the feeling I should be doing something else plagued me for many years along with the odd nudge I received from the universe. In the course of my work, I visited many clients and properties, and I always knew if something was amiss with the site and especially with the clients.

I was used to my hands becoming hot in the presence of someone who was sick or ailing, and now I developed an intense sense of smell when I was in proximity to people with cancer. This, added to my knowing, was very hard to bear. What should I do? How could I say anything? People would think that I was crazy.

These sensations were always there, and I was increasingly desperate to find a way to help these unfortunate people. I was in a taxi on the way to the theatre on one occasion, when I smelled the now familiar odour of cancer and retched uncontrollably in the back of the cab. The driver, a small, rotund man with rosy cheeks and a bright paisley waistcoat opened the windows, turned, and said, "You got it then? You must be a good healer!"

I was flabbergasted and said, "Me? No!" Later, on reflection, I thought, "Maybe that's what has been missing all these years. Perhaps I should find out more about this healing stuff." On return to the stresses of running a business, it was put on the back burner for another day. It remained there until one sunny Saturday afternoon, when there was a knock on the door. My neighbour, who had in tow a tall, black-haired man with intense eyes and horn-rimmed spectacles, greeted me. "I would like to introduce you to a good friend of mine who wants to meet you," he said. I took an immediate dislike to this smiling guy, but for the sake of neighbourliness, invited them both in for tea. Our neighbour explained that his friend was a well-known healer, which I railed at and said that I did not believe.

Mel responded by putting his hand on my chest and saying, "It's wake-up time."

Energy coursed through my body, and my world as I had known it disappeared forever.

"Maybe you should go out into the garden," Mel said.

Resisting the urge to punch this arrogant man's face, I went. My lungs bubbled as the nicotine deposits from my smoking dissipated, and I burst into uncontrollable sobs. As I regained control, I was struck by the enormity of what was happening. What would all my friends and business colleagues think? What would happen if the Rotary Club ever got wind of this? I resolved to keep it to myself while I figured out what to do.

For the next three months, Mel was a constant presence in my life, corded to me whilst I needed him. He often phoned me from New York, where he had a healing clinic, to say such things as "You had a bad night, didn't you?" Then he would talk me down to a calm state. Trying to live amongst two different realities was too much, and I was beginning to doubt my sanity.

On one particular occasion, Mel arrived unbidden to the loading bay of my business just as I was about to completely melt down. I had thought that he was in the States at the time, but he said, "You need me. I'm here."

We borrowed the keys to my secretary's house, just round the corner, and he gave me healing. I gradually saw things in perspective and took control of myself. The next day, my secretary came to work and said, "You owe me for thirteen light bulbs." When she had returned home that evening after my healing, she found that every light bulb in the house had blown!

"If that is the power available through healing," I thought, "then I must learn to focus it myself.

Mel and I remained in contact for a short while, and then he said, "My work is done. You can stand on your own feet now." He departed once more for the United States.

Once I was left alone with my thoughts, I had second thoughts about this psychic stuff. Was it just autosuggestion, and had I fallen prey to a big con? As if to answer my question, for the next four nights in that moment between wakefulness and sleeping, commonly called the alpha state, a stocky, white-haired man with a smiling demeanour and a cigarette visited me. He said his name was Henry, and he had been a printer. He had wanted to be a politician, but fate had decreed that he should be a healer. He also said that I should go with it and help others wherever I could. Initially, I thought that it was figment of an overactive imagination, but when he came back night after night to reiterate the message, I was reassured.

More than two years later, when I was well on the healing road, I was lent a book about the life of a great healer. There, looking bold as brass on the front cover was a picture of Henry in a white coat. He was called Harry Edwards, and it was definitely the same man. On reading the book, I found that he was not only one of the most famous healers of his day but also the former president of the National Federation of Spiritual Healers, with whom I was training. This confirmed to me that I was following the correct path.

My next teachers were soon presented to me. I had made a few enquiries about healing and discovered that once a week, a couple in the next town hosted lectures on varied subjects of an esoteric nature, and I resolved to go. With some trepidation, I slipped into the rear of the gathering and took stock of the audience. I had expected to see weirdos and New Age hippies, but everyone looked normal enough. Over the weeks, I attended a variety of interesting talks and became firm friends with the hosts, Keith and Marguerite, who were kind and most welcoming. They were long-term members of the National Federation of Spiritual Healers, both having held high rank in the organisation.

I was nonplussed at one of these lectures when a middle-aged lady sidled up to me at the end of the evening and said, "My guide is most insistent that I tell you that you will be a powerful healer. Do not falter."

"Oh dear!" I thought. Maybe my assessment of the audience had been flawed.

Nevertheless, this group was just what I was looking for, so I enquired about how this healing stuff worked. As our friendship developed, Keith and Marguerite invited me to join them to learn how to meditate, and I found this practice most helpful. Eventually, they invited me to train as a healer, and I took over three years to complete my training and qualification. It felt good to be able to help.

Within a few weeks of my qualifying as an NFSH healer, fate played her hand once more at a lecture I attended on the subject of the vibrational frequencies of colour. I was seated next to a guy that I immediately warmed to, and in conversation, we discovered that he was a fireman, as were my mother, father, cousins, and uncles.

When he said that he was a Usui Reiki master, I could not believe my luck. In the course of my healer training, I had become aware that there were other forms of energy healing, and my interest had been drawn to the Japanese discipline of reiki as taught by Doctor Usui. It used a method of attunement and symbols, placed into the energy fields of students, to raise and focus their energies. I was fascinated at how the energies used in healing could be channelled, and I soaked up all the knowledge that I could lay my hands on. I could handle this discipline because it wasn't psychic, just energy.

When I was offered the opportunity to study reiki with this kindly man from the lecture, I embraced it with open arms. Over the next few years, Andy, for that was his name, and I became good friends. I absorbed the techniques and attunements and eventually became a Reiki master, which serves me well to this day.

As my client base expanded and my sensitivities grew, I became aware of a whole plethora of various energies. I realized that the world is made up of a great melting pot of vibrational frequencies. Maybe this was why I had been aware of feelings and emotions in inanimate objects such as places and properties for so many years. Perhaps I could learn to interact with these energies—but how?

The Dowsing Solution

It wasn't long before the universe presented me with an answer. I was having dinner with a doctor friend, and he produced a book called *Are You Sleeping in a Safe Place*, which described earth energies and how to find them with bent coat hangers. I was fascinated and immediately bent two metal hangers. To my amazement, it worked.

I spent many years from that moment on, visiting every house, monument, and religious building that I could find. I learnt how the energies flowed and how to determine whether the frequencies there were harmful or positive. I used the rods together with my healing work and site visits not only to ascertain the health of my clients but also to take account of where they lived and worked.

It became apparent that their health was invariably affected by their environment, and that man-made energies could also have a devastating effect on their immune systems. The outcome was, as I had suspected, that problems were due to the effects of vibrational frequencies. My client base continued to grow with requests for house surveys, and dowsing became an imperative part of my work. My dowsing developed to enable me to use the rods as a tool for a myriad of unconventional things, such as sick building syndrome, finding water, archaeology, gas, and underground anomalies as well as lost pets, people, and keys.

I even got the contract to do a site evaluation for the new chalk Folkestone White Horse that was to be cut into the hill above the new Channel Tunnel terminal. The enormous horse, nearly fifty metres high, would continue the age-old tradition of creating sculptures of animals and folklore figures, by removing the turf to expose the white chalk beneath. It was to be set on ancient energy lines in the same way that our ancestors had.

After much research and studying of out-of-print books, I realized that although the times had changed, the earth energies had not. I spent several days hanging by rope onto the steep side of the hill, located the energies that existed, and then pegged out the site, setting the horse in the correct position, to benefit from the ancient earth energies that were present. It was completed in exactly the same way as our forebears had done with other large hillside carvings around the UK.

There was an energy vortex at the heart centre of the horse, and a time capsule, filled with a selection of items that were commonplace at the time, was to be buried there by the local community. It was considered to be a perfect way to show future generations, the way we lived. The project captured the minds and imagination of the national press, and the *Saturday Telegraph* devoted a two-page colour spread to it. This kick started my career, causing requests for consultations and visits to flood in from around the world.

It was simply impossible to visit every site around the globe, so I undertook surveys using map dowsing. This enabled me to remotely view a place and the occupants in question to establish whether a problem existed or not. In this way, I could use my time to best advantage and often avoid expensive travelling costs for the client.

As I honed my skills and became more proficient, I detected strange energies which I could not explain but which had a profound emotional effect on me.

I spoke about this to my mentors, Keith and Marguerite, when we met for our regular meditation, and a knowing glance passed between them. They pointed out that after all the years of work and development, I was making contact with personalities that had died and were still trapped on this earth. This was the very thing that I had resisted all of my life, but now it seemed the most natural thing and I was no longer afraid.

From that point on, they slowly introduced me to a world parallel to our own and gently helped me develop my abilities. Our weekly meditation took on a new form, and I experienced mind-blowing exposure to the other realms in a most unexpected way. We were sitting quietly together one day, meditating in our normal way, when the atmosphere changed and the air crackled with what felt like supercharged energy.

Marguerite's breathing changed, and she appeared to be subtly changing her posture. Suddenly, she sat bolt upright with her eyes wide open and said in a broken English voice with a heavy French accent, "Good evening. We wish to welcome you, and we hope that what you learn will be of use to you."

I was amazed and confounded. She was a long dead nun, who knew that I was there and was speaking directly to me! The atmosphere was warm and supportive. Even though it was a completely new personality addressing me, not Marguerite, I felt at ease. Over the next months, I looked forward to our weekly messages and the knowledge that they presented.

Every pronouncement that she made had a theme, sometimes obscure but always full of wisdom, and I came to respect the conversations. What would she take as a theme this week? I knew that it would be inspirational and uplifting.

Marguerite was a transformational medium, and she was connecting with her guide, a straight-laced, formal, and often very prickly French nun. I had never heard of this practice, let alone experienced it.

Keith and Marguerite had quietly been helping lost souls over to the other side for many, many years. Now, as their student, I was to benefit from that wealth of experience. I was honoured to work with them onsite and in the privacy of our meditation.

Our circle of three contacted many poor souls, lost or frightened, and helped them to the light whenever we could. The scope and diversity of our contacts over several months amazed me: a man who had fallen into a volcano crater, victims of a road accident whose violent deaths had rendered them confused, and some individuals who simply did not realize that they were dead.

On one particularly sad evening, we encountered many people who had just been involved in a major rail crash in southern England. They homed in on our beacon of light in the darkness, shocked and confused, and we did all we could to assist them. We created a column of white light over the scene of the carnage, and many souls gravitated to it and moved into the other realm. I particularly remember one poor deceased lady who desperately tried to find her mobile phone in the wreckage so that she could assure her son she was okay and would be home soon. There was also a deceased smartly dressed businessman who refused to leave the wreckage until he could locate his briefcase that he assured us he would be requiring later. It took me many weeks to come to terms with the pain of this tragedy, and I seriously considered whether I was cut out for this type of work. I soon realized that if I could help in any way, I should, regardless of how it made me feel.

When we went onsite together, I was encouraged to use my dowsing skills to pinpoint the location of lost souls. Marguerite then took position in the centre of the energy and transfigured into the shape and personality of the entity. Keith would then address him or her, and we took what action we could to assist the being's passage to the light. I shall never forget the sight of Marguerite standing in the centre of a large and imposing Victorian house, transfigured into the stooping figure of a grumpy old man, complete with knobbly walking stick and a string tied around the waist of his trousers.

We worked together in this way, and still do on occasion, for many years. I began to make contact with lost and earthbound entities in the course of my work with geopathic stress, or earth energies, using dowsing rods and my fast-developing third eye, or pineal gland.

I went to a lecture about flower sentience one day because I had little else to do. I took my seat in the corner of the back row and watched, barely interested, as the proceedings unfolded. The audience was predominantly women who sat, clutching a flower of their choice and awaiting a reading from the speaker. After she spoke about how their choice of flower would assist in the production of a personal appraisal, I was less than impressed.

The lecturer had thoughtfully provided someone to talk to the remaining audience as she left to chat with those in attendance, one by one, in a nearby room. I was immediately struck by the new speaker's presence and drawn to her energy. I listened with only half an ear to what she was saying, thinking how nice it would be if I could escape to find a cup of tea.

Suddenly, she broke off and directed her gaze at me. In a loud voice, she asked, "You used to have a liver-and-white spaniel, didn't you?" After the shock of being singled out receded, I agreed but asked how she could possibly know that. "Because she is sitting at your feet," replied the speaker. "Could you spare me a few minutes afterwards?" she asked. I was hooked and nodded compliantly.

When the lecture was over, she approached me and said that she knew all about me and my work. She told me of her plans to build a veterinary hospital within a small hospice village so that terminally ill patients could spend their final days peacefully, in contact with animals, and in a caring environment. She requested that I visit the site to check it for suitability and hopefully to situate it on positive energy fields to further support sick animals and patients. How could I refuse?

I soon learnt that Nannette was yet another gifted psychic, sent at the opportune moment in my development to help me along the road, and we became firm friends. We worked together on many difficult and troublesome cases over the years, and I learnt to be detached so that I didn't succumb to the pain and trauma we often dealt with.

We kept separate notes on every job and only compared findings when the work was finished. This enhanced my confidence in my abilities, and I was safe in the knowledge that I was correct in my approach.

I grew in demand as a ghostbuster. To my surprise, I was able to help these poor unfortunate people, and I will continue to do so as long as I am able. It is a privilege and an honour, and I thank the universe for choosing me. Even though I resisted for over thirty-five years, it got me in the end.

The rest of this book chronicles adventures and case studies together with a few anecdotes and explanations. I hope that you will find it interesting, amusing, and sometimes poignant but never boring.

Part Two

Ghostly Snippets

Before we delve into the realms of the psychic and supernatural, it is important to lay to rest the preconceptions with which we are constantly bombarded. The entertainment industry would have us believe that the world is full of dangerous entities—vampires, zombies, and all manner of frightening creatures—which are all out to attack us and wreak havoc wherever they can. After many years working in this field, I must say quite categorically that I have never, ever experienced any of the scenarios portrayed in the entertainment media.

Ghosts Are Nothing Like That

There are, however, cases of poltergeist activity that are invariably triggered by the fantastic levels of energy generated for a short while, as children pass through puberty. These energies can give rise to all sorts of temporary physical phenomena, but these experiences are not caused by cogent entities (i.e., real personalities), frightening though they may be to the uninformed. I shall deal with this topic more fully later in the book.

When we physically die, our souls—our personalities or whatever you wish to call them—leave our physical bodies, which can no longer support them for whatever reason. Normally, we then move to the other side. Now and again, a soul will choose for some reason or other not to go to the other side, and it will instead remain here and become an earthbound spirit.

A soul is made up of pure energy and can be perceived in several forms. For example, it can be seen as a ball of energy, and I have experienced it as a streak of light, but it is often encountered in earthbound form as a double of the body that it once inhabited.

These people without bodies, as I prefer to think of them, often manifest in clothing that they formerly wore. I have, however, seen them change clothes, hairstyles, and colouring when they feel it is appropriate for those perceiving them. Sometimes they can only muster enough energy to manifest the upper portion of their bodies. When energy is in really short supply, they can only be perceived as a presence without form. This can, in its own way, be just as effective.

As Isaac Newton propounded, energy cannot be created or destroyed, and in order for a being to manifest in any form, energy must be found. Therefore, temperatures in the vicinity of a manifestation drop because energy is extracted from the surrounding air.

When working alone, I use a voice-operated tape recorder tucked into my top pocket because I know that I will not be able to recall events accurately later, having been in a different mind-set. This works very effectively when undertaking normal dowsing work, but when I work with ghosts, they drain the batteries of energy for their own use.

Healing does not require the provision of personal energy, simply the ability to channel energy from a higher source. Dowsing, however, can be very tiring from projecting one's energies to contact the target. Ghostbusting is even more exhausting and debilitating, considering your target is intent on using your energies to manifest! I'm always ravenously hungry when I have been on clearance work. I need a good night's sleep afterwards, to replenish my energies, and a couple of days away from this type of work.

Why Do Ghosts Choose to Remain?

For a long time, I wondered why any soul would choose not to cross over. However, the more I made contact with ghosts, the more I understood about the reasons they chose to stay here.

When the time comes for an entity to cross over, the personality and life lessons that a soul has absorbed during its time here remain. Thus, a grumpy old man remains a grumpy old man; a caring, considerate person will remain that in the next world. What I have learnt from souls over the years is that they all have the free will to proceed or not, and their decision is inevitably coloured by their beliefs or lack thereof.

Whilst all souls have very personal reasons to remain, the following are many of the motivations that come up time after time.

- They are afraid to face their maker because of something they did in their life. The brigade of pastors and clerics who preach of a punishing God convinced them that they would be sent to hell or purgatory. As they see it, they choose to remain in this world out of reach of retribution.

- They are frightened of meeting someone on the other side who they do not like or with whom they are at odds. Often it is a girlfriend, ex-husband or ex-wife, or increasingly a business partner or someone that they have cheated or robbed.

- They stay to be with their life partner because they cannot bear to be parted from him or her or because they want to continue to protect that person.

- They stay because of the strong pull of grieving relatives on this side, thinking that their continued presence will be of help in the bereavement process.

- Many who were murdered will not cross over until their killers are brought to justice.

- Souls that were cheated or taken advantage of in some way resolutely stay in an effort to get revenge on the perpetrators.

- Souls that meet a violent end, such as in road traffic and other accidents, are often stuck here simply because they cannot recognize that they are dead. The event happened so quickly and unexpectedly for them, and they cannot understand why no one will talk to them or recognize their existence.

- Those totally addicted to substance abuse often hang around drug dens and bars, looking for a body to inhabit so that they can continue to enjoy the pleasures of alcohol or drugs.

- When a soul enjoyed a comfortable existence in a beautiful and happy home or garden, it is no surprise that it would want to stay there rather than to head off to places and worlds unknown. I have dealt with many ghosts who, at the time of their deaths, gravitated to places where they had their most happy times, whether a home, tavern, theatre, or landscape.

- Some people find themselves bemused when they die because the possibility of a life after death was not part of their beliefs when they were alive. They think that because they feel so alive, they cannot possibly be dead. If anyone tries to help them—angels, guides, or deceased relatives—they simply think that they are hallucinating.

- They stay because they are afraid of losing the status and identity that they built up in this world. They may have been a pillar of the community or a prestigious golf club or whatever.

- And then there are those beautiful souls who lived an exemplary life, often helping others, but still have such a deflated sense of their own self worth. They consider themselves unworthy of a place in heaven and choose to remain.

The ghosts that I meet, in the main, are those that simply need a kind word and a gentle point in the right direction to find their way home to their loved ones. However, as in life, there is a minority of souls who are as stubborn and opinionated as they always were. These hold out as long as possible until someone like me comes along and threatens, cajoles, and points out the error of their thought processes in staying here. It ain't always easy!

Do You Have a Ghost?

When potential clients first contact me, complaining about problems in their house or on their property, I always fill out a comprehensive questionnaire with them. This gives me an opportunity to tune in and establish exactly what might be amiss.

As the years pass the problems are often more complex than they were in the good old days. The problem may, of course, be a ghost, but it could just as well be caused by earth energies, electromagnetic or magnetic fields, poltergeist activity, embedded memories, or any frequency-based problem such as mobile phone masts and microwave equipment. It's getting more complicated every year.

As I said previously, ghosts need energy to manifest, and today's maelstrom of energies of all sorts can only assist the paranormal. I have even seen a television set which was haunted—a perfect source of energy for any self-respecting ghost.

I always make a remote survey of the situation before visiting a site so that I am prepared for whatever might occur. An old saying says, "You only get what you can handle," but in my experience, "Forewarned is forearmed," is more accurate, and I need to know that my guide will be there to assist if needed.

If the situation will likely be difficult to resolve, I often feel the animosity of the ghost when I make a remote survey, and then I can be pretty sure that it knows I am coming. I can always feel anger and resentment building as I travel towards the site, and I become quite nauseous as I approach. On one occasion, I even experienced a ghost dog being projected by the entity to put me off. I saw it as I travelled down a dark, wooded lane towards a haunting. The black-and-white

Border collie stared and ran across my path, right under the car's wheels, but there was no impact. When I got out to check for damage, there was nothing. No dog existed. This was the beginning of a very difficult case, which I will discuss more at a later point.

So how do you know if you have a ghost? Firstly, if you have only one ghost, you are lucky! Only ghosts that want to be alone choose to inhabit a house on their own. In most cases, they often hang out in the same vicinity as other ghosts.

If you are lucky enough to have a portal in your house, you are doubly blessed! A portal is a connection between both worlds, that enables spirits who have already crossed over to travel back and forth freely whenever it is open. These spirits should not be confused with ghosts, who have not yet crossed. It may be under the control of a keeper on the other side to ensure that undesirables do not use it, but that is not always the case. I distinctly remember a portal on the upstairs landing of a house that was similar to traffic in London at rush hour! A portal is not something to take lightly, and I strongly recommend that you have nothing to do with Ouija boards, which seek to open up a connection with the other world. Worry not. Portals like this are not the norm!

Ghosts can let you know that they are there in many ways, and it's not normally intended to frighten you. It's just a cry for help and acknowledgement.

Many of the signs that ghosts will use include:

- Knocking on walls or rapping that seems to come from the inside of wooden cupboards or panelling.
- The sound of footsteps, often on the floor above or below you.
- You feel someone touch you or breathe on you, but no one is there.
- The doorbell rings but no one is there.

- Appliances such as radios, televisions, kettles, turn themselves on and off.
- Water taps turn themselves on.
- Music can be heard with no obvious source.
- You feel someone sitting on the end of your bed or couch.
- Books and decorations are knocked off shelves and tables.
- Voices can be heard, but no one is there.
- Possessions, such as clothes, are moved from one room to another or thrown out of cupboards.
- There is a definite cold spot in the room, but there are no drafts.
- Your house has been for sale for a long time, and despite many viewings, no one has bought it.
- Children say that they can see a person that you cannot.
- You get pushed to one side or pushed downstairs.
- Doors open and close by themselves.
- A mist appears in the room.
- The room is filled with the scent of flowers.

This is not a definitive list, but it's enough to start with! I feel that the best way to know if a ghost is with you is to feel it and then talk to it. It will be grateful for your acknowledgement of its existence.

Part Three

Ghosts I Have Known

For the following chapters, I selected what I consider to be some of the most interesting of the many jobs that I have undertaken around the world. I hope that they illustrate the diversity, and often complexity of the problems that dowsers and psychics are called upon to deal with in the course of work.

It seems to me that it is a requisite for a ghostbuster to be, first and foremost, a diplomat. What these earthbound souls experience is just like normal life, but they no longer have the constraints of their physical bodies. Initially, this can be a problem, as they are often confused by the freedom that they have from the physical laws that constrain us mere mortals. To be able to relocate in the blink of an eye or to travel through walls without problem may be our fantasy, but when it is actually possible, it can be very disturbing and disorienting to a new ghost.

One must play the role of an empathetic advisor, as you are dealing with a wide diversity of people who need to be understood and led into the light, using whatever techniques are appropriate. It is never quite as straightforward as one might imagine.

The Old Schoolhouse

This case illustrates how the good energies and embedded memories of a property can attract ghosts who were associated with it when they were lost and seeking refuge or as a place where they enjoyed good times.

Set in the middle of Kent was a small, picturesque village, looking exactly like the images adorning the top of chocolate boxes and biscuit tins. It snuggled amongst the fruit orchards and hop fields as it had for centuries. Life went on, barely noticing the goings-on in the real world, century after century. It was complete with a village pub, shop, and school.

The local school had been shut many years previously as young families gradually deserted the village for the bright lights of the neighbouring towns. There were not enough children left to warrant its continued operation.

The building, once the pride and joy of the local population, had fallen into disrepair and, except for a brief period in the Second World War, had remained unoccupied. So when a young family expressed an interest in its purchase in the mid-1980s, the local authorities could not wait to get rid of the responsibility of the derelict building.

The family set about restoring the building and, after many months of backbreaking labour, moved in with great excitement. They had restored the property to its former glory, with white walls and a dark-red Kent peg-tile roof. It fitted perfectly with the rest of the village, and the addition of a white picket fence to the front was the icing on the cake.

The couple and their two young children felt that the building was welcoming them. The atmosphere was one of warm happiness. After several weeks, the children talked about their new friends, with whom they played in their bedrooms. They described in great detail girls dressed in bonnets and crinolines with lace-up boots and boys dressed in knickerbockers typical of the Victorian era.

Their parents thought that their children had vivid imaginations until they began describing the games that they had played with their new friends. They spoke of tops, checkers, charades, and blind man's buff, but no trace of these toys could be found.

The parents accepted this, as the children were very happy, and life proceeded. As warmth and energy returned to the long-empty building, other phenomena appeared. The sound of young voices could be heard, melodically singing children's songs and hymns in all parts of the building, and childish laughter rang out from empty rooms. The sound of a hand-held bell could be heard, summoning long-gone pupils to their lessons, often in the morning and the early afternoon.

The final straw for the long-suffering parents was when they heard German marching songs on the ground floors whilst they were tucked up in bed for the night. This was where I came in. I visited the property and found that although the energies in the house were positive, memories of days gone by were embedded in the walls.

The two children that the new owners' youngsters has seen and played with were indeed local and had perished, along with their parents, in a house fire in the village in Victorian times. They had been asleep when the fire consumed them and, being frightened and confused, they had gravitated to their happy place.

I quietly spoke to them and gently asked if they missed their parents. They said that they enjoyed playing with their new friends but wanted to be with their mother and father. They had tried to find them before but couldn't. When I asked them to look around, they could see their parents waiting for them, as they had been for more than a hundred years. There was great happiness, and I watched them disappear into the light, once more a united family. It brought a tear to my eye.

Further investigation on the ground floor led me to a crossing point for positive energy lines, and I found the souls of three German soldiers. They told me that they had been prisoners of war, billeted in the old schoolhouse. They had worked as farm labourers in the surrounding fields for the duration of the war, picking hops and apples in the summer and helping local farmers in the winter. They were a friendly bunch, and they also regarded this building as their happy place. On their demise, they had all gravitated back to their friends and the place where they loved to sing their marching songs together.

I reminded them that although they were enjoying themselves, they had loved ones on the other side who missed them terribly and were waiting for them, so they really ought to go. Being the honourable soldiers that they were, they stood to attention, made the Nazi salute, and disappeared into the light.

After I cleansed the building of its embedded memories, the clients were happy with the results. They are now enjoying a happy family life without visitors.

The Apartment That No One Wanted to Rent

This story demonstrates that we all have an innate sense of the presence of ghosts, although we may not be able to recognize it at the time.

There was an elegant, four-storey Georgian town house situated in what was once an upmarket street but was now but now slightly shabby. Situated in a coastal town in the south-east corner of England, the properties along this street were formerly the homes of the well-to-do. The houses were constructed of local flint from the chalk cliffs of the area and had grey slate roofs set behind decorative parapets with sandstone copings. They also had elegant front steps with servant's quarters in the basement. The wrought-iron decorative railings had been removed as part of the war effort to produce munitions. All that remained, protruding from the sandstone wall of the front elevation, were rows of stubby iron teeth.

Over the years, these fine houses were gradually converted into apartments as the owners fought to meet the ever rising tide of maintenance and repair bills, and this particular house was no exception. A single, somewhat eccentric man had owned the property for many years. He chose to live alone in the rambling house and was a devotee of Esperanto, spending a large amount of his time and effort into promoting what, at the time, was hailed as a language that would eventually be adopted by the whole world. Sadly, this dream would never come to fruition, but he doggedly continued on his path. He was in the habit of helping people who were down on their luck.

One particular night, he invited a homeless person into his house for a warm bed, hot food, and respite from the winter cold in his normal way. With the rising of the sun the next day, the tramp left the house, taking with him all of the cash and valuables he could find. He left the poor unfortunate owner strangled and devoid of life, hidden under a pile of mattresses and bedding in a top-floor understairs cupboard.

Here the unfortunate man's body lay for many weeks. The neighbours did not consider his lack of appearance in the street untoward, as he was a frequent traveller in pursuit of his Esperanto interests. They simply assumed that he was away on another trip.

Eventually his demise was discovered, his estate was settled and the property put on the market. Developers purchased it and converted it into four apartments, which were put up for rent with a local estate agent. The accommodations were in great demand, and eager renters snapped up all available flats in a matter of weeks—that is, except, for the ground floor apartment, which stayed stubbornly empty despite being viewed by fifteen potential clients.

The estate agent soon approached me and asked me to visit to ascertain if there was some reason for this lack of interest. As I drove up to the property, I was aware of a face staring out of the front ground-floor window, with a gaunt and sad expression. As I entered the building, I became aware of a terrible odour, which I quickly realized was psychic and not physical, and I was immediately drawn to the front room on the ground floor. I later discovered that the previous owner had used it as a sitting room.

Standing with his back to me, peering out of the window, was the murdered man. At first I could not reach him, as he seemed remote and locked into his woes. When I finally connected, he told me that he was so sad that his life had been ended in the way that it had. It had stopped his crusade to introduce Esperanto to the world.

I had expected that he was hanging around to see his murderer get his just desserts, but he was simply a man who had lost his focus and didn't know what else to do. He said that he was the only one of his family still on earth, and his seemingly altruistic habit of inviting tramps and ne'er do wells into his home was simply because he sought company in his loneliness. It took little persuasion to pull him out of his introspection, and he was more than happy to go towards the light, where his mother waited for him.

Two days later, I had a call from the estate agent. He was delighted, as the first couple that he showed the flat to after my visit signed up on the spot and had already moved in!

Bleak House Ghosts

This is a story of happy associations with a place and lifestyle and the return after accidental death to the place where it happened.

Bleak House was a typical imposing Georgian property, standing alone atop a hill overlooking a picturesque village in Leicestershire. Affluent farmers of the time had constructed houses like this for themselves, and it was surrounded by an arboretum of specimen trees, that the original owners had painstakingly collected over many years.

The house had its own well, and it was of a size to have required domestic help to keep it functioning. With the demise of its original owners, it had passed down through several generations of the family, finally ending up in a dilapidated state. The house was eventually put up for public auction.

The people who purchased it set about the complete restoration and enlargement of the original property. This major project took almost two years to complete, and the builders often reported unpleasant energies while working in the original portion of the house.

When the new owners finally moved in, they too were aware of unpleasant feelings and energies. Several of their visitors were convinced that they had seen or felt ghosts, so I was called in to check out the premises for anything that might be detrimental to the new occupants. The first discovery I made was a negative energy field flowing deep below the well. I effectively blocked this with earth acupuncture to restore the positive vibrational frequency of the water.

When I entered the old part of the house, I became aware of a female entity residing in the front bedroom. She said that she had been the mistress of the house and had spent a long period before her death in bed, suffering from emphysema. The figure was dressed in a warm flannelette nightdress, complete with woollen bed socks, and she looked wan. Ghosts often revert visually to a period when they were well and healthy and clothe themselves in their finery, but this woman appeared in the form from when she had died. She was loathe to cross over on her demise, preferring to spend her time gazing out at the beautiful view which she had enjoyed so much during her protracted illness. We had a few gentle words together, and she disappeared into the light to be reunited with her husband.

On the ground floor was another ghost, who had met an untimely end whilst working as a maid in the house. She said that her name was Johanna Bellicoe, and I was quite surprised when she told how she had met her end. She had been standing on a three-legged stool to hang a large ham on the metal hooks, which hung down from the roof of the pantry. At the critical moment as she impaled the meat, the stool slipped, and the hook caught in the ring on her finger as she fell, virtually peeling back the flesh from her finger!

She returned to her home on an adjacent farm where she lived, but medical attention was in short supply in those days. She developed septicaemia and eventually died in 1878 at the age of twenty-three. She had been married but had no children.

Having returned to the site of her traumatic accident on her death, she had no knowledge of the passing of time and was most distressed when I mentioned her husband. With a sense of relief, she managed to focus on the light and ran to the arms of her waiting loved one.

You, dear reader, have realized by now that we are eagerly awaited by our loved ones on the other side. When the time comes for us to pass over, invariably they are there to greet us and lead us through the transition with love and compassion. It's a comforting thought!

The clients later contacted to tell me that they were so intrigued after my visit that they checked the parish register in the village church and found reference to the ghosts with which I had spoken. They had also traced the current members of the farming family, who still lived in the village, and they too confirmed the happenings!

They also said that whilst looking through the photographs that had been taken before and after the renovation project, they found a photo of the actual meat hooks hanging from the ceiling in the larder, which subsequently had been demolished.

Flannigan's Irish Pub

Here is a tale of the fear of divine retribution and the fires of hell.

There seems to be an Irish pub everywhere I visit around the world.

I had a call from the boss of Flannigan's Irish Bar at a ski resort in Zell am See in Austria. He was having trouble with his staff members, who were convinced that there was a ghost in the upstairs dance floor and bar area. They refused to work in the bar or to go up there after the evening was over to clear up the effects of whatever riotous party had taken place.

I was unconvinced that the fears of the staff were not being caused by excess alcohol intake, and I must admit that I dragged my feet. Only after the boss kept phoning me, pleading for help, did I reluctantly agree to visit.

The bar was situated in the lower two floors of an old, derelict hotel, which had been scheduled for demolition for many years. It was the typical Irish bar, with large television screens placed strategically around the walls to attract sports lovers for special events.

The bar on the bottom floor, where most of the action happened, was a smoky, dark place with high stools around the bar and the obligatory tree trunk in the corner for the nail game that is so popular in Austrian bars. This involves driving large nails into a block with one blow of a hammer. The loser buys the next round.

The employees were convinced that they saw a dark form, flitting to and fro, in the shadows on the first floor, where all larger gatherings were held. I climbed the dark service staircase from the lower bar to the dance floor. In one corner of the room was the raised stage for the musicians, and on the other wall was a long bar. The end wall was set back behind a series of brick arches. Light levels were, as usual, set to a low level to create the desired ambience.

As I entered the room, I felt my pulse race, and butterflies paid my stomach a visit. Although the room had been in use that same evening, it was now icy cold. I, too, distinctly saw a dark shadow flitting across the room behind the arches. Then I realized that I was not alone. Huddled right behind me in a tight knot were the complete bar staff and the boss. I was not used to working with such a large and obviously frightened audience, but what the hell?

Even with the energy of the frightened group obvious behind me, it was apparent that the ghost, pacing back and forth behind the arches, was also in a state of some anxiety. It was a strong-looking man of about forty-five years of age with a weather-beaten face. He was dressed in a white shirt with the collar turned in, a black jacket with two rows of silver buttons down the front, and a black felt hat with a wide, flat brim. He had a cloth bag slung over his shoulder and carried a cane made of a twisted branch. A single decorative earring dangled from his left ear. I moved towards him, asking him not to be afraid and telling him that I only wanted to help. He told me that he had been a journeyman carpenter from Germany, and he had worked on the construction of this hotel. A wooden scaffold had collapsed, and he was killed. He had absolutely no concept of time.

When I asked him why he had chosen to remain rather than pass over to be with his family on the other side, he said that his priest had told him throughout his life that if he led a flawed life, when the time came, he would go to the fires of hell. He had been paid in cash for his work, and was frightened that this would consign him to the fires of Hades, as he taken the vow of poverty required by his guild.

We talked for a while, and I told him that the only hell was the one that he had created for himself, in his mind. If he were able to set this to one side, he would be able to see the bright white light around him. He tried and almost immediately said that he could see it and was being drawn into it. I wished him well, and he was gone!

Most of my audience was also gone after deciding that it was no place for them and retiring downstairs. I found them huddled quietly together, staring with anxiety into the bottom of large glasses of schnapps! Nothing I could say would persuade them that they had been in no danger, but I suspect that the real problem was that they had been faced with certain knowledge of the existence of a hereafter which they could not deny. When presented in this way, it is not an easy matter to process!

Further research revealed that the term "journeyman" was in use from the Middle Ages onwards. They belonged to various guilds, which often required adherence to a specific moral code. They were obliged to travel and work abroad for a minimum of three years and a day and to contract themselves to various companies for periods of six to eight weeks before moving on. They could only take with them their tools and whatever they could fit into a canvas bag. The clothing that the ghost wore was typical of a journeyman and denoted his status as a professionally trained carpenter.

Grandma and the Poltergeist

Read the unbelievable story of a pubescent teenager and her grandma's ashes!

A large Victorian house in an affluent part of a cathedral city in Kent was the scene of this unlikely drama. The house was, like many in the street, very large, and the top floor had been converted into a luxury apartment, which was rented out. The remainder of the property was a comfortable home for an affluent and well-connected family. The family consisted of mother, father, and two children: a boy of eleven years and a daughter in her mid-teenage years. The children both attended private schools as day pupils. The daughter was headstrong, and as she approached puberty, she became rebellious and difficult to handle, often staying out at night and mixing with a dubious peer group.

A recalcitrant grandma further exacerbated the family problems. She had always been difficult and outspoken, and she loved to kick over the traces. Indeed, this was not only her declining years, as she was widely known to have cavorted with RAF pilots throughout the war years. In order to give everyone a little peace, she was moved between her three grown children on a regular basis, spending a few weeks and then being passed from one unwilling family to the next. When she finally passed away, the whole family heaved a collective sigh of relief, cremated her mortal remains, and got on with their lives.

The family life resumed in this Victorian house, but soon they began to experience strange goings-on, especially when the daughter was in residence rather than out clubbing and generally trying to follow the example of her deceased grandma! Doors opened and slammed of their own volition, lights went on and off, and books and magazines were strewn around. The focus appeared to be on the first floor, where the daughter's bedroom was. The family asked a local bishop they knew to visit to see what he could do. He visited, said prayers to demand that the spirit leave, sprinkled holy water around, and pronounced the problem solved.

The next day, the problems worsened and the cold water stopped coming from the pipes. They called a plumber, but he could find nothing amiss and left the house dumbfounded. The tenants of the top-floor apartment expressed surprise, as they still had water flowing from their taps. This situation was patently impossible, as the whole house was fed from one pipe.

The family asked if I could identify the problem, so I visited the site and was met with a very belligerent daughter. Uncontrolled energies were flooding from her aura in a way that suggested that she was experiencing the transition from childhood to adulthood.

I asked to see her room, and as I entered, an aerosol hairspray can lifted vertically from her dressing table, flew horizontally across the room, missed my head by a few centimetres and attempted to embed itself in the door lintel! The dent in the woodwork was enough for me to realize that, had it met its target, it could have caused me a very sore head.

Convinced that this was poltergeist activity stimulated by the uncontrolled energies of the daughter and not a spirit or ghost, I spent quite a while telling her my thoughts and asking her to try to contain the outbursts of emotion and unjustified anger she was directing at her distraught parents.

However, not convinced that I had understood the situation correctly, I searched for further sources of energy that could possibly be contributing to the phenomena, but I could sense no ghosts or spirits. I located what appeared to be a portal of a transient nature located in the cellar and went down to investigate. I was led to a small room at the back of the basement, where I found an urn nestled amongst the old paint and brushes. Although not open at the moment, the portal was positioned around the urn.

When I spoke to the parents about the urn, the mother said, "Oh my God, I forgot granny!"

She explained that when the woman had passed away, they were so relieved. When the urn was collected from the undertaker, the plan was to have a family gathering to spread her ashes at sea at her request. Unfortunately, a member of the family was abroad, and they had decided to wait until everyone was present. The weeks had passed and turned into many months, and the urn was placed in the cellar, awaiting the ceremony that never came.

I suggested that the ceremony be completed with all haste, and the next day they hired a local fishing boat. The grandma's ashes went to their final resting place. When the family returned to the house after the ceremony, they were amazed to find that peace had been restored, the water was flowing freely once more, and their daughter had been restored to them. She was still a typical difficult teenager, but they decided that, in comparison, to past events, they could easily cope with that.

I returned to the house and cleansed it, raised the energies, and burned sage, and to this day I have received no further contact from these clients.

The grandmother had been coming back through her own portal to show her anger at the predicament of her ashes, and she had supplemented the daughter's energies to enhance the phenomena.

The Psychic Surgery Saga

This is not a ghost story but a tale of how I was persuaded for once in my life not to be so inquisitive and headstrong when something new was presented to me.

The healing practice was established, and I had a strong and growing client base. I had opened a complementary therapy centre, which we called The Priory Centre because it was adjacent to the twelfth-century Priory of St Mary the Virgin in Dover, and everything was going well.

One day, I was working with a patient who had a back problem. My hands were working on her spine when I had the strange sensation that my fingers were getting longer and penetrating the skin. The client immediately sensed this and said it was strange that it felt like my fingers were around her spine.

I was shocked but said nothing, and the session came to a normal conclusion. A few days later, I worked with a gentleman who had shoulder problems, and the same feelings manifested. He was delighted and expressed his gratitude as the shoulder softened and released. I was very concerned, as I did not understand what had occurred. I was very relieved when the phenomena did not return again, and I settled back into my normal treatment regime.

Several weeks later, my daughter phoned me to say that she had seen an announcement in the newspaper that a well-known psychic surgeon was due to appear at a local bookshop that evening to promote a new book he had written. I expressed an interest, and she said that it was almost certainly fully booked at that late stage, but she would phone the shop in any event.

When she phoned me back, she was very confused. The bookshop had told her that the event was full. Then the assistant asked her, "What is your name?" After hearing her name, the assistant said, "I have two seats reserved in that name. The tickets will be waiting for you at the door." But we had not ordered them!

As the evening drew closer, I became more and more intrigued. We took our seats in the back row with an air of expectation. The surgeon continually made eye contact with me as he emphasized point after point in his presentation.

When the meeting concluded, we made to leave, but the author stopped me and asked me to remain until the audience had left, which I did. When we were finally alone after his book signing, he said that he recognized my energies and that we would be seeing each other again in the near future. I left, clutching a signed copy of his book. My inquisitiveness was most definitely aroused.

Three weeks later, I received a telephone call from the secretary of the surgeon, who said that the man was scheduled to be on tour in Europe in two weeks' time and had received late notification that while he was abroad, a coach full of people were due to arrive in his clinic in Chelmsford. Would I please go to the clinic and treat them?

My mind was in turmoil. So, that was what all those strange feelings had been about. Some higher power had scheduled me to be a psychic surgeon. I was in two minds. Part of me wanted to know more, and another part of me was afraid of being used in such a way, so I told the secretary that I would take some time to consider my options.

My teachers reminded me that I always had free will, and I should follow my innermost feelings. Ultimately, the decision was made for me a few days later. I had been treating a well-known local psychic called Pam for a while. On this occasion, she sat up bolt upright on the couch and said, "You must not go, you know. It is not for you." I had told no one of the request, but she knew all about it.

In my usual impetuosity, I decided that I simply must go to Chelmsford to see what it was all about. However, the other side had different ideas! Two days before I was due to go to Chelmsford, I was working in the garden with my son. It was a beautiful sunny day with not a breath of wind, and we were replacing two-metre fence panels. The garden was set two metres higher than the road outside and was contained by a heavy flint retaining wall. On top of this wall was a high fence to prevent debris from the wooded area behind it from falling into the road.

I was standing on this wall with a panel in my hands when a heavy gust of wind suddenly came through the dense foliage of the trees behind us, lifted me into the air still holding the fence panel—now acting as a sail—and deposited me flat on my back in the road, two metres below. The fence panel landed on top of me.

When the panel was lifted, I asked? "Where did that wind come from? It's very lucky that I did not hurt myself." After I stood up, although I was in no pain, it was obvious that the lower part of my left leg was broken.

I visited the hospital, still without feeling pain of any sort, and an X-ray confirmed that I indeed had two spiral fractures of my left lower tibia. A friendly doctor put a plaster cast on the affected area and made an appointment for me to revisit to ensure that all was well.

I was obliged to cancel my imminent journey to Chelmsford and felt a little disappointed that I would never know what had been in store for me there. I returned to the hospital for the follow-up ten days later and had another X-ray. The doctor apologized when he read the X-ray and said that the wrong leg had been screened as there was no sign of the spiral fractures.

I confirmed that it was indeed the correct leg and the technician had made no mistake. He examined the film more closely and said, "You are correct. I can just see the lines of the breaks, but they are completely healed. That's not possible in just ten days!" Neither the doctor nor I could understand it.

The plaster was removed, and I proceeded home with a wry smile on my face knowing that I had been pointed back into my correct path once again whether I liked it or not. After this experience, I decided that I was not comfortable with psychic surgery work, and I was never troubled again by such an injury.

I know that the story sounds fantastic, but I assure the reader that events actually happened in exactly the way I have described them.

The Stone Street Highwayman

Read the story of an unfortunate man who was hanged as a highwayman, decided to stay here, and liked it!

When the Romans invaded Britain, they built a harbour on the southern coast called Port Lympne. The sea later reclaimed this area which now forms the Romney Marshes. Port Lympne is no longer connected to the sea, but the road that the Romans constructed to connect the port with Canterbury still remains. These roads were constructed in a straight line from one place to another as far as was possible, and they were paved with stones. Therefore, it is not surprising that they became known as Stone Street in many locations.

Over the centuries, these roads became the prime routes for travellers, and in the seventeenth century, a coaching inn, called The George" was constructed beside this particular Stone Street. The inn was of typical Kentish construction: timbered walls, in filled with soft red bricks and topped with a roof of Kentish peg tiles. There was a large barn to the side of the inn, which was used as a meeting place by the local population for everything from barn dances to magistrates' courts.

I visited the inn several hundred years after its construction to try to assist the current landlord experiencing problems that he could not explain. His bar staff turnover was considerable, with very few lasting in his employ for more than a few weeks. They all reported total terror when going down into the cellars to change over empty beer barrels. Their identical stories claimed that when they were in the cellar, they immediately began shivering with an ice-cold draft, and someone tapped them violently on top of their heads.

In the bar area upstairs, on several occasions, water dripped through the ceiling above, behind the bar and onto the head and arms of the barperson. Glasses were seen to move through the air in full view of everyone in the bar. When a plumber lifted the floorboards in the room above the bar, he pronounced that a leak was impossible because there were no pipes there.

The inn had a typically rustic bar with a timber-beam ceiling and a big inglenook fireplace in which always burned a welcoming fire. This area was so big that the locals could and did actually sit in it on cold winter nights, gathering around the blaze with a cheering glass of porter. The original stools that had been there for hundreds of years still remained and showed signs of the scorching by the roaring fires of many a day.

One particular stool in the dark recess at the back of the inglenook had, over the years, become a talking point and was seldom if ever used. On the grimy top of the stool, the words "Nathanials's stool" were scratched, and a story had grown up around it. Supposedly it had been the stool of a long-deceased local who had frequented the hostelry. The landlord, ever eager to increase his takings, actively encouraged this story, and the regulars often drank toasts to Nathanial in a friendly and frivolous way.

There was no sign of a ghost in the pub when I visited, but I felt strongly that someone's soul often visited. This is not uncommon in pubs and taverns, as souls that enjoyed a drink in their previous lives often return to see if they can hitch a ride with someone who is drunk to relive the pleasure that they used to feel.

I was drawn to the large barn attached to the tavern, and the embedded memories of the events that had occurred there over hundreds of years were readily apparent. In one corner, I contacted the ghost that I suspected I would find there. He was a man of middle years, dressed in the simple farm clothes of the eighteenth century with a very prominent rope burn around his neck.

He told me the story of his demise in a very matter-of-fact way. He had been a local farmworker and a regular visitor to the inn. One day, he was walking to the tavern, to enjoy a pint when he saw a leather purse in a ditch. It contained a few gold sovereigns. Putting it into his pocket, he continued on his way. Unbeknown to him, there had been a spate of highway robberies on Stone Street, and he had found the highwayman's stash left for collection when the hue and cry had quietened down.

Whilst enjoying himself at the bar, he inadvertently pulled the purse from his pocket and was immediately pounced upon and pronounced the highwayman that everyone had been looking for. Despite his protestations, the magistrate was called. In the rough-and-ready justice typical of the time, he was summarily declared guilty and hanged in 1756 from one of the beams in the barn.

He was a devout Christian. Fearing that he would not be welcomed into the next world because he was hanged, he had chosen to stay in his favourite pub, sharing the atmosphere and enjoying the ambience in a quiet way. The phenomena had simply been his way to let people know that he was there; he had meant no harm. When I told the landlord of my findings, he was more than happy to let Nathanial, remain in his happy place. I put no pressure upon him to move on, having told him that he had free will and could cross over whenever he wanted to.

I visited the same pub several years later, and there was a new manager. He said that when he first arrived, the cellar was still a problem. But to their surprise, when their first child had arrived on the scene, everything stopped and the atmosphere improved dramatically. Nathanial obviously loved babies.

The Ghosts of Conquest House

This is the story of the Cavalier, returning from the war, and his unfaithful wife!

Conquest House in Canterbury has a long and colourful history, beginning in the twelfth century. Whilst it is hard today to imagine it as an ancient building when looking at the beautiful late-Tudor or Jacobean façade, the house contains a wealth of features lurking behind the half-timbering. For example, a fourteenth-century Norman undercroft and highly decorated seventeenth-century fireplace seem relatively modern when compared to the twelfth-century original.

The walls contain a plethora of embedded memories, accumulated over many centuries, which I found hard to bear when I first entered. Emotions flew about in all directions.

In 1170, four knights met in the undercroft of Conquest House to plan the murder of Thomas Beckett, the archbishop of Canterbury, having had a fruitless argument with him over the excommunication that he had placed on several of the king's supporters. They were trying to curry favour with the king, Henry the eighth, who regarded Becket as a thorn in his side, after he refused to carry out the kings wishes. They left the building through a small, arched stone door in the rear of the undercroft, located Thomas Beckett in the cathedral nearby, and killed him after further argument.

The site of Beckett's death is now called "the Martyrdom", and it is in a prominent place in the cathedral. However, I have since made further study of the site and found that he was not killed where the marked site is but deep within the undercroft of the cathedral, where he was attempting to avoid the knights. Moving special sites of interest to give pilgrims easy access to them is a common feature of many religions around the world. (see later chapters for more on this).

I was asked to investigate the house, which was being used as an antiques shop, to allay the fears of the staff that worked there. The story of the murdering knights in the cellar had been established for several hundred years and was of no concern to them. What did worry them was the feeling of being watched within the building, especially as the light faded, and the fear that they found themselves confronted with as they left the building after the day's work was done.

The offices of the antique shop were on the top garret floor, and they constantly felt a presence there. The biggest problem, however, was when they had to descend an ancient winding wooden staircase down to the Norman croft (the main first-floor room) and thence onwards down a further narrow stair to the ground floor. As they descended the spiral staircase and it opened out into the lower room, they were transfixed with a fear bordering on terror whether they were alone or not.

Never before had I been bombarded by so many energies and frequencies exuding from the fabric of a building. I decided to use the traditional dowsing technique of isolating one particular source of energy at a time, totally blocking out everything else. Going to the top of the building, I met a kindly young man who said that he had lived in the garret during his lifetime and had been an ostler (stableperson) in the service of Gilbert the Citizen. He had simply remained in situ when he died and was more than happy to move into the light when I presented him with the offer.

The problem at the base of the spiral staircase was a completely different matter. It was obvious from the intensity of the frequencies and emotions present that more than one soul was there. Focussing in on three ghosts simultaneously was not an easy matter, but I succeeded in doing just that with the two men and one woman that were there.

After a long and emotional conversation, I discovered that the lady, appearing to me in all her finery, was married to the soldier who had been a Cavalier. He was away from home for a protracted period, fighting beside King Charles the First as a Royalist in the war against the Roundheads and Oliver Cromwell. He appeared in typical costume: a wide-brimmed hat, knee-length boots, and a very muddy and dishevelled uniform. He had arrived home, unexpectedly, to find his wife in the arms of another man at the top of the stairs. He made to run the admirer through with his sword, but his unfortunate wife was herself killed in the melee whilst trying to intercede for her new lover.

The wife was filled with anger at losing her lover, the husband was distraught at having killed his wife, and the lover was rooted to the spot from having been the cause of so much anguish. After I explained to them that they had all been souls for many hundreds of years and that no good could be achieved by remaining on the earthly plane, they all agreed to move on. They headed off into the light, hopefully to resolve their differences in another, more peaceful world.

Whilst it was obvious that many other ghosts and energies remained at Conquest House, my brief was to neutralise the presenting problems. No doubt in the fullness of time, someone will be required to examine the structure in depth, but that task had not been laid at my door.

The Nackington Ghost

Here is one story of how a new house can be haunted with the ghosts of the past when it is constructed on a previously used site.

There had been a farm at Nackington for hundreds of years. When it was finally sold in the 1980s, it was because the demands for high-class housing could only be met by expanding the city into the countryside. Land prices had risen to such a degree that the farmer could make more money by putting the proceeds of the sale into investments and living off the interest without all of the backbreaking toil of an agricultural life.

The farm was developed into an exclusive private community with six very expensive houses built in the classic timbered style popular at the time. People at the upper end of the housing market instantly snapped up these attractive properties.

The problems began not long after the purchasers of the central property moved in. This sat almost directly on the site of the former farmhouse, and the original well was rebuilt to form a feature on the front lawn to enhance the carefully contrived ambience.

As the house absorbed the energies of the family and become more than new bricks and mortar, the owners got the feeling that they were not alone. They were the traditional family: mother, father, one daughter, and one son, and the daughter first raised the issue of feeling watched, especially when she was in the bathroom.

The father was out of the house a great deal on business, and when the children were at school, the lady of the house was often alone for the greater part of the day. She began to feel that someone was standing behind her as she sat at her study desk, writing, so she moved her chair and desk so that she was sitting with her back to the wall. To her horror, she then sensed someone breathing in her ear. The final straw was when the bedroom door began to open at night, when her husband was away on business.

She contacted me, but I was working abroad at the time and could not visit for another eight days. By the time that I arrived, the house was in complete turmoil and matters had taken several turns for the worse. The initial feeling of being watched had developed to such a degree that the daughter refused to sleep alone.

The mother had laid out her clothes on the bed on one occasion and gone to take a shower. When she leant out of the shower to take the towel from its place close by, it had vanished with all of the other bathroom towels! She was obliged to leave the bathroom without clothes to get spare towels from the linen cupboard. When she returned to the bathroom, all of the towels were back in their usual place. Returning to the bedroom, she found that the clothes she had laid out were no longer there, and she was obliged to select a new outfit. The clothes appeared two days later in a spare bedroom, neatly folded in a pile on the floor.

The man of the house was very dismissive of the problem when he arrived home after a long day at the office and was met with two hysterical females. However, he was somewhat chastened when they went into the kitchen to eat their evening meal, only to find that the cooker master switch, a heavy-duty control unit, had been turned off and the prepared meal was uncooked.

Having ordered a Chinese meal to be delivered, they set the table with cutlery for the imminent arrival of their supper, and the adults poured a glass of wine to relax their nerves. They were sitting at the dining table discussing the recent events, when a knife began to move. It went in a 180-degree arc around the plate and placed itself, wrong way round, beside the fork on the other side of the place setting. That was it! Within five minutes, the whole family left the building and spent the night in a local hotel, returning only when the sun rose the next day.

Initially, my search revealed no ghosts or spirits present, but the energies suggested that there was indeed a soul paying occasional visits. I left, promising a return visit the next day, as the light was fading and I prefer to work without the primordial fear of darkness that we all possess impinging on my energies.

When we met the next morning, the lady was very agitated. She had been taking the children to school that morning, and on the journey home, she was aware that someone was with her in the car. The electric windows began to operate on their own, and the radio turned itself on and off. She immediately stopped the car, locked it, and made her way home on foot.

My rods led me out of the house and onto the front drive, where I met the ghost. He was a young man who had worked on the farm. He was hitching up a pair of working horses to the heavy cart used on the farm, and the animals got spooked and reared up. He was caught underneath their legs and met his death in a very quick but painful way.

As is seen often when someone meets a quick, accidental death, he was lost and disorientated, and he was stuck at the scene of his death. He could not understand why people did not notice him, but when the new house was built, he was attracted to the female energies. He seemed to be a bit of a ladies' man and was enjoying the effect of the phenomena that he had been creating.

When I told him that he was, in fact, dead and had been for quite some time and explained that he would be much happier in the next world, he apologized, turned, and walked into the next world.

I visited the site several months later to advise on why the well was dry, and I learnt the family had had no further unexplained occurrences.

Richard J West

Incidentally, the well was dry because the amount of water extracted for the needs of the local population had doubled, and the water table had dropped dramatically. I recommended that the well should be dug deeper by twenty-six feet to reach the lower water table!

The Haunted Gardener

This is the story of someone who was subjected to all manner of unwanted psychic attention by a mentally disturbed person who was not dead but very much alive! Whilst not a ghost story, it serves to illustrate the power of mental energies and how mental abnormalities can open the door to the lower elements.

I was approached in September 2006 by a gardener who told me that he was experiencing strange phenomena. He was middle-aged and lived alone He was in apparent good health, as one would expect from a gardener who worked outdoors in all types of weather. He showed an intensity of personality, but I concluded that this was because of his anxiety.

The gardener lived in a ground-floor apartment of modern design in a good quality building that was approximately twenty years old. He complained of a very intense smell of stale urine, which appeared every evening at about 8.30 p.m. in the corner of his lounge. At this stage, he was more inquisitive than concerned as to its source.

I visited him to ascertain if there was, in fact, a physical cause, more as a parapsychologist than a physic. One must always investigate and discount the normal before looking for paranormal explanations. I firmly believe that any psychic work demands a grounded approach for it to be credible. I could find no physical explanation or any evidence of ghosts or psychic intrusion.

Two weeks later, the gardener made further contact with me, saying that the smell was still appearing at the same time and was now following him around the apartment, staying just inside his bedroom door when he retired for the night. He was a little more apprehensive but still not unduly worried.

We made enquiries from the owners of the apartment block, who said that the previous occupant of the space had been an elderly lady, and she had died there. My client decided that as far as he was concerned, this was the cause of his problem, and he no longer required my services. I found nothing to substantiate his assertions. And then in mid-October, I was enjoying a pleasant evening in front of a comforting log fire, when the phone rang at 9.30 p.m. It was the gardener in a funk. He said that he had decided to retire early to bed to read. No sooner had he settled down than he smelled the now familiar odour, only this time it appeared to occupy the unused portion of the double bed beside him. He tried to ignore it and went back to his book.

After reading a few paragraphs, he became aware that there was a presence of some sort standing beside his side of the bed, soon to be supplemented by one on the other side of the bed. To top this, there was a more powerful presence that appeared to be controlling the other two, standing at the foot of the bed.

He was not given to flights of fantasy, and he was completely nonplussed by what was happening. He attempted to rationalise the situation, and then he felt something stroking both his forearms and his face. He heard undecipherable voices muttering all around his bed. When he felt something touching near his genital area, he totally panicked and was about to decamp to a hotel for the night when he called me.

I told him that it was not my practice to work at night because of the fear response embedded in mankind's DNA. This adds another facet to be overcome and makes psychic work even more difficult than it normally is.

We had a lengthy discussion in which I advised him on self-protection using egg breath and other techniques (more on this in a later chapter), and he felt empowered enough to remain in his apartment. I told him how to approach any further phenomena and said that he could reach me at any time should he need to. He went back to bed.

The next morning, he phoned to say that at 2.00 a.m., he had experienced another attack of the touching and the unintelligible babble. He had, as I had instructed him to, turned on the lights and said, "Go away. I do not want you here." The noise of the babbling increased and then was gone. Greatly relieved, he went back to sleep, only to be roused one hour later by the same situation. That time, he turned on the light and waved his arms in the air as he repeated the agreed-upon words with great forcefulness. He left the light on, and nothing further occurred.

I agreed to revisit the apartment later in the day. Nothing untoward was in evidence in any of the rooms other than a definite altering of the vibrational frequencies in the air, which produced an audible hum in the bedroom. There was no geopathic stress or any magnetic or electromagnetic field problems evident. There was similarly no residual evidence of cogent psychic intrusion (i.e., ghosts). I had to expand my area of search, as the phenomena my client experienced were typical of low-grade elementals that would normally need some sort of portal or vehicle to manifest in the earthly plane.

After a while, I became aware of a focus of disturbed energy outside the gardener's apartment. It was centred on the apartment, directly opposite his front entrance door. It transpired that the woman who lived opposite his door was a middle-aged woman suffering from immense emotional problems. She had been complaining to the building manager of a smell of stale urine over several months, and people regularly heard shouts and screams emanating from her apartment. She lived alone and did not make eye contact with any of the other tenants or even acknowledge them. She had a manic demeanour, and it was obvious—confirmed by my guide—that her disturbed state of mind had been enabling demonic forces to use her as a channel for intruding into the earth plane.

I protected my client's apartment and raised the frequencies by smudging, burning incense, and doing positive rituals of several types. I expanded upon and reinforced the self-protection rituals with him and gave him a Seraphus Bay spray for his further protection (also explained in the chapter on protection). On his return home, he reported a noticeably lighter atmosphere and a return to its feel before he was bothered. I expected that that would be the last I heard of his matters, but I was wrong.

The gardener worked extensively for a local hotel, formerly a Victorian boarding school with large gardens that had been converted. My client had a dedicated storeroom for his tools and equipment. It was under the roof in the attic, of all places, dedicated for his sole use. There were only two keys, one for him and one for emergency access. The emergency key was held by the manager, locked securely in the hotel's safe.

The day after I protected the gardener's apartment, he called me at 9.00 a.m. and implored me to meet him at the hotel. We went, with the duty manager, to his storeroom. The manager said that guests had reported noises and banging in the attic the previous night.

On unlocking the door and entering the room, I was met with a scene of total disarray. Brooms and other long-handled implements were propped across the doorway to hinder access, and everything had been displaced. Items were removed from boxes and packing cases and strewn around the room. The gardener's spare clothes had been screwed up and hidden under a pile of spare beds, and his shoes were thrown deep into the corners of the exposed roof space. The pièce de résistance was a large metal spike, which no one had seen before, driven into the brick chimney breast. It was 400 millimetres long, and it proved extremely difficult to remove from the wall. The gardener was extremely frightened by this turn of events and took more than a little calming.

It appeared that, having been deprived of their playground, the elementals had turned to the gardener's other private space to wreak their revenge. It took me quite a while to protect the space from their intrusion.

A few days after these events, I learnt that the poor unfortunate lady who had unknowingly been the catalyst for these phenomena suffered a complete psychotic breakdown and was moved into secure care. As far as I am aware, she remains there to this day.

The Unpaid Housemaid

The ladies in this story knew that items were being tidied away but didn't realize that they had a housemaid who had been doing it for over three hundred years.

There was a beautiful seventeenth-century Kent clapboard cottage set in a remote spot on the Isle of Oxney, now part of the drained Romney Marshes. It stood proud, as it had always done, dressed in its white timber planking and topped with a soft-red peg-tile roof. It had square leaded windows and a quaint weather porch over the front door to protect it from the fierce storms which often swept over the marshes.

The house had settled over the three hundred years of its existence, and it now sagged slightly towards the centre, which only added to its charm. The inside was just as charming, with exposed timbers and an inglenook fireplace. Its owners, two ladies in their middle years, were antique dealers and interior designers who had lovingly restored the whole property. It was full of delightful antique furniture and bric-a-brac to complement the welcoming effect.

The women did not notice the problems that eventually came to light for the first two or three years of their occupation, as they lived in something of a mess as they restored their cottage. They balanced that with the demands of their antique shop in a fashionable London suburb.

They had been misplacing things and put it down to tiredness and the stress of commuting. The problem really became apparent when the lost items began turning up in odd places. For example, they found clothes in the log store, food items in wardrobes, and plates and cutlery under the beds. The accidents that occurred on several occasions when they descended the tiny, steep staircase from the upstairs bedrooms were the final straw. The women suffered several sprained wrists, turned ankles, and bruises. They put this down to the steepness of the stairs until they both realized that on every occasion, they had received a hefty shove from behind, which unbalanced them and made them fall.

When I paid them a visit, I was impressed with their calm approach and their deep-held conviction that nothing bad existed in the cottage. When I investigated, I found the house warm and inviting with no cold spots or other indications of a ghost. Having satisfied myself that all was well, we all sat down to tea and cakes, which is one of the positive sides to ghostbusting. I was just about to indulge in a scrumptious-looking scone full of cream and strawberry jam, when I felt an uneasiness creep over me, and the temperature dropped by several degrees in a matter of seconds. I grabbed my dowsing rods, and they led me to the bottom of the staircase, where I became aware of a female presence that had descended the stairs.

I tried to contact her, but she turned and fled back up to the rear bedroom. I followed her and became aware that she was in her mid-twenties. She was a simple soul, without malice, who was simply frightened and confused. Whilst I tried to elicit further information, she turned and disappeared though a curtain in the corner of the room which I had assumed was acting as a clothes cupboard.

On pulling back the curtain, I saw a small winding stair that led up into the attic, where the young woman was cowering in a corner. She was obviously terrified, and it took a while to convince her that I meant her no harm. She was consumed with the fear that she would be evicted. Rather than upset her further, I decided to use my dowsing rods to find out what had happened to her.

Note: Dowsing is an invaluable method of obtaining information, as one can easily go back in time to obtain accurate results. One can also find the long-gone footprints of old buildings and events. This is a boon to archaeologists in their search for historical artefacts and sites.

I found out that the cottage had been a family home in the 1750s, ringing with the happy voices of several children and their parents, who had a small farm in the vicinity. The house was bursting at the seams, and one particularly dark and stormy night, they had found the girl lying in a ditch in the lane outside their home, cold and wet. Without a second thought, they took her in.

Before the family found her, she had been evicted from the cottage that she had shared with her father until he died. She was thrown out to make way for the worker who was to replace her father. She was left to fend for herself, as was common in those days, and she struggled to survive. Life was hard in those times. The family had made up a bed for her in the attic, the only place left in the overflowing cottage.

She remained there for several years, free of any rent, and all her needs were met. She repaid their kindness by undertaking any chores that needed doing and became a valued member of the household. Eventually, the hardships and privations of her earlier life caught up with her, and she died. She was interred in the local cemetery, but her soul remained in the only place that she had known love and kindness. She continued, over the centuries, to help whenever she saw a need. The girl seemed not to notice the regular change of occupants until the ladies arrived and changed her home out of all recognition.

She wanted to remain and help as usual, but she had absolutely no grasp of the modern world, hence placing items in inappropriate places. She had no idea that she had caused hurt on the stairs and explained that she just wanted them out of the way so that she could, as she perceived it, get on with her work.

I spoke to the young woman gently and told her quietly that she could, if she wished, be reunited with her father. She brightened at the prospect. Once I explained to her that she only had to look around, and she would see the light, she did exactly that, and with a whoosh, she was gone! No further problems have been reported at this house.

The Ties That Bind Us

As I mentioned earlier in this book, the emotional bonds that we forge with family and friends can be a powerful force in the decision of a soul to remain on the earthly plane. The following stories illustrate that this can apply not only when we die but also before we choose to die.

It was a typical semi-detached house on a typical 1940s street in the coastal town of Folkestone. There was nothing to distinguish it from the hundreds of other bay-windowed properties in the long avenue that looked out over the English Channel, but as I approached it, I felt an overwhelming sense of sadness. As I drew my car to a halt, I was aware of a presence staring out of the upstairs bay window, as often happens when one's imminent arrival is expected. This phenomenon occurs regularly, as by various means, a ghost is aware of an impending visit and reacts in one of several ways. Normally, there is a feeling of resigned calm or relief, but I always know when the visit is unwelcome. I take extreme care not to blunder into a situation which could be difficult or dangerous without first consulting my guide to ensure that I am capable of resolving the situation alone. I always ask can I, and should I? Do I need help? If a positive response is not forthcoming, I will take a rain check until another day.

On this occasion, all of the occupants of the house were happy to see me. Over the usual cup of tea, the situation became clear. The mum was of middle age, and she had lived with her two daughters for the last nine years since the demise of her husband. They had been a very close family, sharing the ups and downs of life together. When the eldest of the daughters succumbed to depression amidst the stress of gaining a university degree, they closed ranks and attempted to help her through it. It was to no avail, however, and she took her own life with an overdose of barbiturates.

The remaining daughter and mum were completely distraught. Try as they might to move on, they were completely unable to, constantly saying that they wanted the other sibling back. This is normal in the grieving process, and it struck a chord with the deceased daughter. Still in the lower astral plane, she felt that she had deserted her loved ones for whom she cared so much.

The mum and daughter both became aware that the sister had returned to be with them and was constantly by their side. Initially they found it comforting, but as the weeks progressed and they experienced stroking on their arms and faces as they slept and when they relaxed in the evenings, they realized that matters needed to be resolved for the good of all, especially for the soul of the much-loved daughter.

I sensed that the soul of the daughter who passed away had been with us while we discussed the situation, listening intently to the conversation. It was not difficult for us to verbalise that although she was and always would be much loved, the remaining daughter and mum could manage without her, and she should not stay just for them. We also made it clear that her feelings of guilt for taking her own life should be set aside. We decided to pray for her and wish her bon voyage, and in the course of this, she took her leave and moved to the next world.

The remaining family members took notice of my pleas not to discuss matters for a while and get back to normality, as far as was possible, to avoid calling the daughter back from her new life. After six months had passed, I made contact once more, and life had settled into a new pattern with no further psychic events being felt.

This is a story of passing over delayed by emotional cords.

Whilst working in my healing role, I visited a middle-aged lady client who was terminally ill on a frequent basis. She was in hospital receiving excellent palliative care.

Her husband, who was totally devoted to her, was an aficionado of alternative therapies. When she told him many months previously that she was convinced she had developed cancer, he decided to take care of her in his own way. He took her to every complementary practitioner that he could find, often travelling the length and breadth of the country in an abortive attempt to find a resolution.

Eventually she became so ill that her husband was forced to abandon his search and reluctantly put her into the care of the medical system. He constantly preached the gospel of positive thought to her and held to his belief that she could heal herself.

It was soon discovered that she was in terminal decline with advanced cancer, and little could be done because of the many months' delay in making a diagnosis. Her husband, whilst still in denial, was heartbroken but persisted in his forceful pronouncements that all would be well. He insisted that she must stay with him because he could not live without her.

By now my visits were daily, and it was plain that the poor lady was suffering greatly and could not remain here for much longer. My job as a healer was to aid her transition to the other realm in the most advantageous way for her. It was difficult to see her struggling day after day against insurmountable odds to stay with her husband, when it was obvious that her dearest wish was to pass over and end her suffering.

Whilst I was giving her healing and the husband had left the room for a coffee, I told the woman that it would be fine if she followed her heart and moved into the light to be met with her loved ones. I assured her that her husband would be okay, and I watched her essence leave her body and pass into a better world. It was almost twenty minutes later that the nursing staff confirmed that her body had stopped breathing and she was at rest.

There are countless reports of events occurring in exactly this manner over the entire history of the world. I suspect it will always be so. People who are about to pass over invariably wait until they are alone and their loved ones have left the room before they slip away.

The Gamekeepers Cottage

This is the case of the mother who refused from the other side to sell her house

Hidden deep in the English countryside, in a sunny clearing in the middle of a deciduous wood, was a charming cottage of a former gamekeeper. The positioning of the cottage, down a long track in the centre of his beloved woodland, was ideal for his work. When the man unexpectedly died, instead of throwing his family out of the house as was the norm, the landowner had allowed the family to remain. Over the years, the owner had even allowed the mother, who worked for the estate, to slowly purchase the property.

She was a devoted and hardworking mum and struggled to bring up her four children—three boys and a girl—but had succeeded against all of the odds. One of the boys had met his demise in his teens by freezing to death overnight on the doorstep, having come home without a key. One of the other boys experienced mental difficulties and was fiercely protected by the whole family.

When the mum finally died after a lifetime of caring for her family, it was not surprising that her one wish was to ensure that they were safe. By this time, the eldest son and daughter had become adults and fled the nest, and the youth with difficulties would now be alone in the cottage. His siblings were of one mind. They could not leave their brother to fend for him self in this remote cottage, and so they decided to sell it. This would provide a nest egg for their brother's care payments in the future. They set to work with a will to restore the cottage from its dilapidated condition into an attractive and saleable proposition.

When they were finished, it was a rural ideal, with its neat cottage garden, brick front path, and white picket fence. Inside, they gutted the property and decorated it in bright and welcoming colours, including white walls and bright-yellow woodwork. The sunlight flooded in onto the newly laid terracotta-tile floors, and everyone, especially the estate agent, was convinced that it would be eagerly snapped up.

Whilst renovating the cottage, the children had been aware of a presence watching over them. They were convinced that it was their mum, happily watching them set up a financial future for their brother. How wrong they were!

As soon as the For Sale sign went up, she realized their intentions were to dispose of the cottage. This was when the problems began. The atmosphere in the cottage became cold and menacing whenever prospective purchasers arrived, and the mum did her utmost to dissuade any people viewing the property from going up to the bedrooms. She gave them a hefty shove back down as they attempted to climb the stairs.

The newly installed central heating system refused to operate despite many visits by the engineers, who could find nothing wrong. Additionally, the main power switch was constantly turned off. Prospective purchasers who arrived at the cottage full of enthusiasm had no sooner stepped over the threshold than they were subjected to such aggressive frequencies that they turned on their heels and fled as fast as their feet could carry them.

When I received the call to visit from the children who were now desperate, it did not take long to realize that their mum was at the root of the problem. As I drove down the long and winding track to the cottage, with trees overhanging and dappling the sunlight, it should have been idyllic, but the familiar butterflies in the pit of my stomach began to flutter. I knew that whomever I was going to meet would not be happy to meet me.

On entering the cottage through the weather porch, I was immediately assailed by the mum and a blast of icy air in my face. She did not want to talk to me, but I persisted. I enlisted the help of her children, and we formed a combined front. We explained out loud, in no uncertain terms, that although she thought that she was looking after her children's interests, she was in fact preventing a solution for their problem. She paced up and down on the ground floor whilst we talked, and it was all that I could do to keep up with her. She was a strong personality, as she had been in life, totally convinced that the plan in her head was a viable one. When she turned and made for the stairs, presumably to get away from my attentions, I made to follow and received a shove for my trouble.

Finally, I made her understand that all her hard work for her children was not about to be wasted. By disposing of her beloved house that no one now needed, she would actually continue to give them the support that she always had. As the atmosphere slowly changed and the sunlight flooded through the tiny windows, she realized that her work on this side was done. When she saw her gamekeeper husband strolling across the clearing to his front door as he always had, she walked out of the front door, linked arms with him, and disappeared into the sunlight.

Within the next two months, I received a letter from the daughter, telling me that a buyer had been found and her brother's future was assured.

The Ghost in the Orchestra Pit

This is the story of a musician in medieval times who travelled from one cathedral city to another, performing for the pilgrims.

For several hundred years, devotees made pilgrimages to the cathedral cities of Great Britain, such as Ely, Winchester, Wells, and Canterbury, to name a few. They worshipped at the shrines and enjoyed the mystery plays that were very popular at one time. This attracted all types of people, not just pilgrims, and the cities became a melting pot of street traders and entertainers, all looking for an audience.

The subject of this particular story was a street musician in the seventeenth century. Together with his comrades, he spent many months of the year travelling around the cathedral cities, entertaining pilgrims with madrigal music, a particular form of harmonic singing. They also performed with the musical instruments of the time, such as a lute or cittern, in the cathedral precincts.

Our friend, who had his home at York, was often on the road for many months at a time. He missed his wife and two children greatly. His nomadic life meant that he and his fellow travellers did not eat properly and often spent their nights roughing it in some barn or outhouse, a routine which was not conducive to good health. His fondness for alcohol exacerbated the situation. It was not surprising, therefore, that he contracted typhus, a disease transmitted by lice, which was extremely prevalent in those days, because of the lack of hygiene. He was struck down by the illness whilst entertaining pilgrims at Canterbury.

When he died, he was alone in a strange area with no friends to speak of, and his soul wandered aimlessly around the city. Eventually, he took refuge in a place that seemed welcoming and full of like-minded people whom he hoped would understand and befriend him. This was the Marlowe Theatre—specifically, the orchestra pit—which was only a few hundred yards from the city's cathedral.

He tried to make contact with the resident musicians without success. The musicians, however, reported not only shivering-cold spots in their cosy pit but also the feeling of someone breathing over their shoulders whilst they were playing. At first they laughed it off, but when they felt someone gently poking them, they had had enough. That was where I came in.

This ghost seemed greatly relieved when we made contact. He said that he had been unable to converse with anyone, despite trying everything that he could to get their attention! When I pointed out that he had been stuck on the earthly plane for a very long time and that he could, if he so wished, be reunited with his beloved family, he was delighted. It took no more than a few moments to show him the light and his wife and children waiting for him, and he ran quickly to the new life that awaited him. He was another happy soul!

The Vibrational Frequency Effect

The next couple of chapters will hopefully demonstrate something of a different subject, which appears with amazing regularity. It is the phenomena of the ever present vibrational frequencies that form an integral part of everything we experience.

The Vicar and the Witch

I was once asked to visit a church vicarage in a village that will remain nameless at the behest of the vicar's wife. She was convinced that something was amiss with the energies of the residence.

As I drove up the impressive gravel drive and swung to a halt outside the manse, I was struck by the beauty of the ancient Norman church, constructed of knapped flint so many hundreds of years ago, which was nestled amongst the trees a few yards away. I resolved to pay it a visit as soon as I had dealt with the situation at the vicarage. It has always been a keen interest of mine to visit ancient churches and structures, not only to admire their beauty and the skill of the craftsmen that constructed them but also to investigate the energies and the forces that make them the spiritual havens that they are.

I was greeted by the vicar's wife and immediately noticed that she did not offer me her hand but simply turned on her heel and ushered me into the well-appointed lounge. Although she was making all the usual social gestures and remarks, she would not make eye contact, constantly wrung her hands in nervous apprehension, and did not come close to where I stood.

Ignoring this, I asked her what she perceived to be the problem and attempted to get a handle on her and her husband. I was met with evasion when I asked about her background and beliefs, but she was more than happy to tell me that her husband had spent many years abroad in the service of the church, both as a missionary and a military chaplain, before being recently granted this parish.

She told me that they had a daughter who had worked in Africa until her untimely murder the previous year. They had only recently taken receipt of the daughter's possessions, returned after many months afloat in a container en route from Africa.

I began my scan of the property and was immediately aware of powerful and malevolent energies emanating from the dining room. On opening the connecting door, I could not believe my eyes. The room contained four wooden carvings of African origin, displaying devilishly leering and grotesque faces with piercing eyes. In the corner of the room was an old wooden box, secured with a crude metal lock. A quick look into the box showed me that it contained the tools of a witchdoctor or shaman. A vibrational frequency of which I had not experienced until that time emanated from the items. It seemed to be trying to draw my energies from me, and I quickly withdrew to take stock of the situation.

The client seemed completely unaffected by these forces but conceded that her husband, the vicar, was affected in the same manner and would no longer enter the dining room. The artefacts, she explained, were collected by her daughter whilst on travels in Africa. Her husband had wanted them left in the outhouse, but she had insisted that they be displayed there.

Alarm bells rang in my head, but I continued my scan of the building. On the first floor, I became aware of another soul. I told the vicar's wife that I wished to investigate further, and she demanded to come with me to see what I had found. This is not normally my way of operating, so I said that she could accompany me only if she allowed me to afford her some protection. This way I could concentrate on the job at hand and not have to worry about her. She reluctantly agreed, so I opened her hand and placed in her palm a few drops of the Christ quintessence which I always carried with me.

The effect was unimaginable and worthy of a Hollywood blockbuster, as though I had placed sulphuric acid in her hand and it was burning her flesh.

She screamed, "What is this? What have you done?"

I said, "It is the protection of the Christ quintessence."

She responded, "I will have nothing of that name here." Muttering obscenities, she fled from the room. I could hear her running her hand under the cold tap in the kitchen, muttering a ritual or mantra. That was a confirmation that this lady was practising the dark arts in some form or other. I decided that I had to finish what I had started, and I went upstairs.

The soul was most certainly trying to hide, and it had taken shelter in the airing cupboard on the first-floor landing! I found out he had been the former incumbent of the vicarage and had been an avid beekeeper. He had decided on his death to enjoy its ambience until his friends, the bees, had been found a new home. This had now been done. He explained that he wanted to move on, as he knew he should, but he was being drained by the dark energies and rituals that were now being performed in the building. I offered him assistance, and with a little top-up from my personal energy field, he found it within himself to move into the light to be reunited with his God and perhaps his beloved bees.

When I returned downstairs to the lounge, the lady had composed herself, and she pretended that nothing had happened. A look in her eyes confirmed that we both knew her dark secret. I wondered if her husband was aware of her interest in the occult but decided that it was not within my brief to intercede.

I recommended that the carvings and artefacts be removed if the harmony of the vicarage was to be restored, but it was obvious that if she had anything to do with it, they would be staying. The client showed me to the door, thrust money into my hand, and assured me that she would be back in touch within a few days. That was many years ago, and to the date of this writing, she has not. No surprise there!

As you will have realized by now, everything in the universe—whether it is a living being or an inanimate object—is made up of a vibrational frequency and can be affected by the surroundings and events to which it is exposed.

The Key West Colonial House

The next story takes us to the other side of the Atlantic for a tale of clashing embedded energies that produced unexpected results.

The town of Key West, 129 miles south of Miami, is part of the Florida Keys, and it is built on an exposed promontory surrounded by the ocean on three sides. Its long and proud history includes a seafaring tradition steeped in the dastardly doings of old-time wreckers and pirates. From the 1800s onwards, the houses were extensively made of wood, often driftwood and shipwreck salvage, and they were typically constructed with covered porches and louvred shutters as a protection against the fierce sun.

Being only ninety-one miles from the shores of Cuba, the area was of prime importance to the navy. They developed a plan to demolish these wonderful buildings and replace them with stormproof concrete structures. Resistance to this plan was high, but one particular Key West resident became a heroine by setting out to preserve what buildings she could before they disappeared under the demolition ball. She was a fifth-generation resident of the island and an avid preservationist of its heritage.

She singlehandedly restored her house, built in the 1830s, and filled it with authentic pieces of furniture to create a museum to the past of Key West. She was a feisty and determined lady, and when she died in 1934, her house continued to operate as a museum.

The problems began when, in an effort to enhance the visitors' experience, inauthentic pieces of furniture and other items were brought into the house. Curators experienced feelings of being observed, and they watched helplessly as the beautiful gold-trimmed sliding doors between the main hall and the sitting room slid sedately open and closed of their own volition. They saw door handles turning and certain pieces of crockery and cutlery moving on the dining table, similarly untouched by human hand. As might be predicted, the former owner had returned to show her anger at the inauthentic pieces that were put into her home, albeit with the best of intentions.

Staff members felt uncomfortable when alone, which they often were, and I visited to attempt a cure. Furniture and house contents each have a vibrational frequency, which tends to balance out over time by proximity to other items. This adjustment results in a harmonious frequency which encompasses everything contained within the structure. Any pieces from another source must necessarily bring with them the diverse frequencies, and indeed emotions, that they have absorbed over time.

It was not a difficult task for me to identify and list the disharmonious pieces in the Key West house so that they could be removed and return the house to its former ambiance. Once the removal was complete, I was informed that all was quiet once again. Peace reigned supreme once more!

As a conclusion to this section on vibrational frequencies, another contract that springs to mind was that of a very wealthy gentlemen who bought a castle in Spain. He employed interior designers to furnish it with all manner of wonderful pieces of antique furniture, paintings, wall hangings, and the like.

The visual effects were stunning, but no one had considered that these pieces, lovingly assembled together, had absorbed all manner of vibrational frequencies from the places that they had been and from the embedded experiences of their former owners.

The clash of energies was so glaring that even the most closed-down persons experienced a feeling of intense imbalance and could not stay there. I spent many hours working through these pieces and eventually harmonised their respective frequencies so that they could be enjoyed together in a peaceful ambience.

The Caribbean Connection

This is the story of a most unlikely attachment from the past.

Hanna and Winston were born on the sunny Caribbean island of Jamaica. They spent their childhood happily playing amongst the palm trees and rolling surf. They were best friends throughout their childhood, and this developed into a deep friendship that lasted into adulthood.

It was assumed that they would be married, but Hanna decided that she wanted to find a new life. She emigrated to England, where she set up home in the sprawling suburbs to the west of London. Having trained as a secretary, she settled down to a single life. For the next twenty-five years, she enjoyed a comfortable existence.

Hanna asked me to call on her because she was aware that something was wrong. When she visited her doctor, he gave her nothing but a prescription for a tonic and instruction not to work so hard. As soon as I visited her pristine little bungalow with its neat flowerbeds and closely cut lawns, it was obvious that something was amiss.

She complained that she felt drained of energy to such a degree that she was struggling to maintain her house and garden to her usual high standard

Hanna said that her creative spark had deserted her. She felt that her usual upbeat character had changed, and some other personality had taken over. In fact, she felt helpless and feared that she was being obliged to make life choices which were not her own—as if she was living out someone else's life plan.

Hanna had at first accepted that it might be something to do with her health and mental well-being, but when scratches appeared on her forearms and occasionally her face, she became really frightened. Having been a God-fearing churchgoer all of her life, she prayed for a resolution to her problems. This granted her a temporary respite, but then everything resumed at a higher level.

I made all of the usual practical checks for geopathic stress, electromagnetic fields, and underground watercourses, but could find no abnormalities. I noticed split-second flashes of anger and resentment showing in her eyes while I worked, and I felt that I was being urged to leave. Instead of going away, I sat her down in an easy chair in the sitting room and placed an empty chair beside Hanna. I asked her to stay calm and clear her mind as much as she could, and I addressed the personality that I felt had invaded her through a tear in her aura. I was greeted with an emotional display, and the soul announced that he wanted to stay with his loved one.

In an effort to relieve Hanna of her intruder, I persuaded him to leave her and take a seat in the adjacent chair so that we could discuss matters. After a while, he complied. Immediately I took the steps to seal the hole in Hanna's aura with a red pomander that affords protection, and I showed her how to further protect herself from future intrusion using a visualisation technique called the egg breath. (see Glossary)

The unwanted visitor was in fact Winston, Hanna's boyfriend of so many years ago. He explained that he had been devastated by her departure and had vowed to make things right between them. He was unable to do that, as she was in a far-flung part of the world, and he had lived out his life lonely and unfulfilled.

When he died and his soul was unfettered, he realized that he could travel instantaneously wherever he wished. He then found his unrequited love and got as close to her as he possibly could. The scratches that he had generated were his way of attempting contact with her, and he deeply regretted the distress that he had caused.

A bizarre conversation between Hanna and Winston followed, with me as a go-between. She told him of her affection for him and said that she had made a difficult choice, all those years ago, to leave and seek a better life, but marriage had never been a possibility for them. He then realized that his life's total focus had been based on an incorrect assumption, and they would only ever be friends. Hanna assured him that their friendship would remain and that she would see him again when she too passed over. In a flash, he was gone!

One very strange facet of this case was the fact that the scratches erupted and subsided on a regular basis, normally twice every twenty-four hours. I was at a loss to explain this until it became apparent that their arrival coincided exactly with planes that passed overhead as they began their descent to London Heathrow Airport. Further investigation revealed that the phenomenon was triggered only by flights arriving from Jamaica. That is something I will never understand.

The Ghostly Voyeurs

I have to include a couple of stories that show that our earthly obsessions and practices remain with us when we pass over. Once a voyeur, always a voyeur!

I was called to a house in a lonely spot deep in the countryside to investigate a particular energy problem the wife of a local farmer was experiencing. They had two girls, who were eleven and twelve years old, respectively.

The dad was out of the house at the crack of dawn, every day of the year, to work on the farm and did not return until late in the day. The girls went to the school a few miles away, where they would remain until their day finished. Their mum, however, spent most of her time alone in the house.

Before the family contacted me, the woman of the house noticed that she was experiencing memory loss and would answer the telephone, only forget who had rung or what was said. She complained of feeling like there was cotton wool in her head, and she was fuzzy and confused whenever she was at home.

Matters came to a head one day when she did not appear at the school to collect the girls at the end of the day. Their father was called and collected them, but when they returned home, his wife was nowhere to be found inside. Looking out of the window, they saw a figure in the distant fields that appeared to be wearing a nightie at five in the afternoon.

It was the lady, and when she was returned to the warmth of the house, she had no recollection of what had happened. The local doctors undertook a raft of tests but could find nothing amiss. After a short spell in hospital, she returned home feeling well.

However, after three days at home again, the symptoms returned, and it became obvious that the house had something to do with the problem. When I visited, I was immediately aware that the energies in the house were awry, but try as I could, I found no answer. My head felt as though it was stuck in the clouds and I found it almost impossible to focus. All of a sudden, this sensation stopped, and everything returned to normal. I continued my search outside and found that immediately adjacent to the house, there was a very deep borehole where the local water company extracted water supplies for the adjacent community. I was looking at the cap of the borehole when the large pumps cut in once more to drag the water up from the depths, and the symptoms returned with a vengeance.

After much lateral thinking, it became apparent to me that the pumps were not only dragging down the water table to pump the water to ground level but also dragging down the earth energies, in a very large manmade vortex. This was making matters very difficult for the area around the house.

After many months of tedious negotiations, this problem came to a head. The water company, unable to close the well or offer any solution, made the farmer a very generous offer to vacate the premises that he and his family accepted. Until the deal was made and the house was demolished, the wife limited her exposure by taking a part-time job in the local village shop, and this controlled her symptoms.

Now we come to the point of this story! In the course of my survey, I became aware that there was a male presence residing in the house. When I mentioned it to the family, the girls said, "Oh, it's only George. He used to live here before we came. He's okay but a bit of a dirty old man. He always watches us in the bath."

Their mother was visibly horrified at this and asked the girls why they had never mentioned it before, but they just laughed. She asked me to put my psychic's hat on and get the man to move on. When I eventually managed to make contact, he was very loathe to leave. He said that he was very happy with his new guests. After I pointed out to him that it was no longer his house, and his wife was waiting for him in the next world, he went, but reluctantly.

I told the family that in view of his reluctance to go to the light, they should not discuss the matter for a while. This would let him settle into his new world. Two weeks later, the client told me that one night at supper, the girls had said, "What a pity George has gone. We really miss him!" As soon as they went for their evening bath, he was back! This time they could even see the outline of his figure through the glass door, and the bathwater became stone cold in only a few minutes! It took another visit to sort George out, and this time I made sure that his wife came to collect him. She was not happy.

Story number two about a voyeuristic ghost occurred in the mountain village of Zell am See in Austria. In the centre of town in a quiet street was a typical wooden mountain chalet constructed in the early fourteenth century. It was a beautiful building that had been skilfully converted into luxury apartments whilst preserving the façade. The only problem was that the former owner had decided to stay. A lady who occupied one of the converted flats said that she was going to have to vacate for the sake of her frayed nerves unless I could help. She told a tale of being watched by piercing eyes, especially when preparing for bed. The woman was convinced that someone was looking in at the window.

She became more and more anxious and was reluctant to undress or take a shower, which was obviously not a situation that could be tolerated for long. She brought a friend to stay, and the friend experienced the same feelings. The final straw was when she experienced what felt like being tucked up in bed by unseen hands, and she moved out to stay with the friend.

I visited, and sure enough, I was met by the former owner, dead for many a year He decided that he, too, liked the new people living under his roof and was loathe to go to the light and miss his regular show of femininity. Eventually, he succumbed to a diplomatic approach and parted for new horizons, where everyone hopes he will remain—especially the lady tenant!

Psychic Snippets

Over the years, I have come across many little events of a psychic nature which may be of interest. Here are a few of them.

1. Haunted Toilets

Believe it or not, over the years, toilets of all sorts have figured in my work I suppose that it's not really surprising, as we all spend quite a lot of time there, but it's not something that we like to talk about.

- The Victorian Toilet

It was a toilet of no particular merit from the Victorian era. The white china bowl was inscribed "Thomas Crapper" inside the rim, topped by a scrubbed hardwood seat. It was connected to a cast-iron, high-level cistern by means of a very long downpipe. A long chain, complete with ceramic pull at the bottom, was used for flushing. This was connected to the cistern, and a sharp tug was required to empty the water from the cistern into the pan below. The problem was that it had a mind of its own.

The occupants of the house heard the toilet flushing itself at all hours of the day and night, when it was obvious that it was not occupied. They installed a lock on the door and sprinkled talcum powder liberally on the floor to catch any prankster, but the toilet still flushed.

They left the door open to try to spot what was happening, but nothing ever did until their backs were turned. After a while, the joke paled, and I went to see what could be done. There appeared to be little amiss, with no lost souls or other elemental forces in evidence, but still it flushed on its own.

There was a teenage boy in the house, high on hormones. This could have caused poltergeist activity, but it was by no means certain that this was the case. The head of the household decided that enough was enough and called the plumbers to fit a bright and shiny new toilet with a different type of flush mechanism, and the problem ceased. The perpetrator was obviously not up to speed with modern technology.

- The Haunted Teashop Toilet

In the centre of the ancient streets of old Canterbury stands a sixteenth-century house. It has been used for many purposes over the centuries, as not only a private residence but also an antique shop. Currently, it serves as a traditional teashop.

During the course of the restorations required to make the teashop, many ancient artefacts were unearthed. Many traditional practices of the past were revealed, including bags of salt in the brickwork beside the hearth and a collection of children's shoes from the 1500s. Children's teeth and locks of hair were also discovered behind old wooden panelling. As the work progressed, temperatures in the building fell, and unusual sounds were heard. The builders made a point of leaving the building before dusk whenever they could. Souls that had inhabited the house and not moved over made their presence felt, and making mischief was the order of the day.

In my experience, objects moving and taps turning on and off are "normal," but the events that occurred in the top-floor toilet here were something else. Patrons using the facility often rushed down the newly restored staircase with faces as white as sheets after they experienced the games being played there.

They all gave the same story. When sitting down in the toilet, they felt a strong pair of hands on their shoulders, holding them down so that they could not rise. When they eventually managed to stand, the ancient catch on the door was firmly held from the other side so that they could not open it. Once the patrons reached a stage of severe panic, the atmosphere would change, the door would be freed, and they could make their escape. I can personally vouch for this story, as it happened to my wife. Who says ghosts don't have a sense of humour?

- The Haunted Auditorium Toilets

There is a major auditorium in London that is well-renowned not only for its international standards of entertainment but also for its plethora of ghosts. Over the years, many psychics have been called in to assist with varying degrees of success. Many stories have been—and I am sure will be—written on these events in the future, but let us concentrate on the job at hand. The staff became more and more fearful when locking up for the night and worked in twos for moral support.

I visited the large men's toilet, situated on the top-floor gallery of the auditorium, at the behest of some of the staff. They experienced extreme feelings of fear and apprehension when they entered the room at the end of the evening performance to turn off the lights. The entrance to the facilities was down a set of four tiled steps, and as I put my foot on the first one, I was met with a wave of anger stronger than I usually felt. Girding my loins and remembering that the best method of protection is not being fearful, I descended the stairs. Before I knew it, I was picked up and thrown back out onto the warm carpeting of the auditorium. This was early in my career, and I felt totally out of my depth, so I decided not to proceed further. Underneath the toilets, on the next floor down, was a staff bar to which we repaired to patch up my shattered nerves. Standing in a circle with drinks in our hands, we were discussing what had just happened, and I said in a moment of bravado, "I'll be back to sort that out." In front of several witnesses, my double brandy simply exploded in my hand and showered everyone with shards of glass. I never went back to that toilet!

2. The Ivybank Conversion Ghost

During the early years of my psychic career, I simultaneously ran a small local building company. We had a contract to convert a large Georgian house into a nursing home on the death of its owner. The name of the house was Ivybank, not surprisingly because it was built on an ivy-covered bank overlooking the village. The family had been in residence for over three hundred years and grew wealthy on the profits of the local flourmill during that time.

With the coming of mechanisation, the waterwheel-powered mill became obsolete, and the family fortunes took a turn for the worse. When the last mill owner died, the crippling estate duties had forced the sale of the ancestral home. Our contract to convert the building involved completely gutting the property and rebuilding the inside to a new design more fitting to a nursing home.

The work began well, but as it progressed, everyone noticed the change of atmosphere but put it down to the building work. The workers began to argue, accusing each other of playing tricks.

Workers misplaced tools, and there was a constant knocking on the front door. This meant that whoever was working in the house at the time had to make the long trek from wherever they were working to see who wanted entry. On opening the door and finding no one there, the worker often heard a knocking from exactly where that person had been working. This happened many times a day and was often accompanied by the overpowering smell of sewer gas. Tempers became frayed, and the activity came to a head not long afterwards.

There was one carpenter working for the firm who was in his late sixties and a no-nonsense trade unionist. He was not averse to stirring up trouble wherever possible. He was a large man with a rosy complexion and a red nose, who appeared to be resting on his sawhorse whenever he could. He regularly began work one hour earlier than the other men so that he could leave early to undertake his union business.

One morning, I visited the site very early and found him in the former dining room, sitting on his sawhorse as I had suspected. This time, however, his face was as white as a bed sheet, his eyes were protruding, and sweat was running down his face. He could not speak, and he was staring at a blank wall. When I finally calmed him down, he said that he was going to collect his tools and would never step foot in the building again.

Sitting outside in the sunny garden, he told me what had happened. He was working at his bench, engrossed in his work, when he glanced up and saw a man materialise through the wall in front of him, shake his head, wag his finger, and then turn and walk back through the solid wall from whence he had come.

The carpenter described a tall man dressed in knee boots, tight trousers, and a thigh-length riding coat, holding a riding crop in his left hand. The man's eyes burned fiercely with anger, and the carpenter felt his knees buckle and his heart pound when the man looked at him. Nothing encouraged him to stay, even the offer of more salary, and he left the company, never to return.

Later that week, the same figure was seen in the middle of the day by another member of the workforce, only this time the apparition stared intently at a large blank wall at the end of the former sitting room.

As the walls were stripped of their old lath and lime plaster, unexpected discoveries were made. At the exact spot where the ghost had passed through the wall was a doorframe that had since been blocked and covered over. He was simply retracing his steps through the doorway that he had used when he was alive.

Later that week, the wall at which the ghost had been staring was stripped, and lo and behold, there were three large sash windows, still intact with glass and curtains, which had simply been bricked up outside and plastered over inside. This must have been a favourite view of the mill owner. From those windows, he could survey the village and his beloved mill. As the work continued, the atmosphere returned to its normal frequency, and calm was restored. The ghost was never seen again.

3. A Personal Collection Service

In many cases over the years, people who call me are convinced that they have been invaded by ghosts, and then I find on arrival at their homes that a member of the family is seriously ill and about to die.

It is quite a common and beautiful thing that loved ones who have already crossed over return to guide and assist their relatives into the light. In my mind, however, this leaves a psychic with the dilemma of whether to tell those who are nursing the sick person what is happening. Over the years, I have almost always chosen to be diplomatic unless I am asked directly. However, my personal experience in this area was difficult, to say the least. A few years ago, I was in hospital recovering from a major operation, and I had been highly medicated for some time. I was recovering well and due to be released the next day.

In the middle of the night, I awoke to find three people at the end of my bed, staring intently at me with quizzical expressions. There was an elderly lady resplendent in a twin set and blue-rinsed hair, a tall and sombrely dressed man in his late seventies dressed in a black suit, and a lady of senior years with lightly rouged cheeks dressed in a floral frock. "My goodness," I thought, "those pain medications are finally making me hallucinate." Then I realized that, for the first time in three weeks, I was medication free. This was no hallucination.

I quickly tried to make contact and realized that it was not me that they were looking for but an elderly friend that they had come to meet. They faded from view, and I dropped back into a fitful sleep. When I awoke refreshed the next morning, I left my room and walked out into the corridor, and the room next to mine had been sealed. The staff nurse said that this was normal procedure when there was a death. The lady in the room had expired in the night. Then it struck me that the beds in adjacent rooms were sited head-to-head against the party wall, and so I had been sleeping head-to-head with the departed lady. No wonder the group had been confused. I must admit that I heaved a sigh of relief that my time had not yet come.

4. Embedded Memories

It is common knowledge that places and buildings can absorb the energies of past events, and the following stories illustrate the point extremely well. The phenomena can present in several ways. They can be visual, auditory, emotional, or a combination of all three.

A good example of a *visual* experience is regularly observed in the basement of a thirteenth-century building on the high street in Canterbury. The cellar is all that remains of the original structure, with the upper three stories having been rebuilt in the eighteenth century. I have had cause to visit it on several occasions to help lost souls and aggressive ghosts who have migrated there.

The property, currently being used as a shop, is built on top of the old Roman road that once existed. Over the hundreds of years since then, ground levels have risen considerably. Even the floor of the basement is more than three feet above the original road surface. This surely explains why, once a year as regular as clockwork, a legion of Roman soldiers can be seen walking through the basement, buried up to their waists in the floor. There is no sound, just the spectacle.

I experienced an example of an *auditory* embedded frequency when I visited the ancient castle of San Cristobel at San Juan, Puerto Rica.

The castle was constructed in 1519, and the cells and dungeons have absorbed memories of so much sadness, torture, and deprivation that it was difficult to ignore. I was in the dark, damp depths of the castle, and I had strayed from the well-lit tunnel into a cul-de-sac.

I found, by the light of my iPhone torch, a small cell that contained beautiful drawings of galleons, complete with billowing sails and tiny figures on the decks. These had obviously been drawn into the walls through a combination of scratches and charcoal by some unfortunate sailors who had been incarcerated hundreds of years previously.

I could feel no trace of their beleaguered souls and made my way towards the light at the end of the passage, when I heard a dreadful sobbing and wailing which touched my heart. The walls of the cell were releasing the embedded memory frequencies of the pain and anguish that those poor sailors had endured. I can only assume that I was able to hear their plaintive cries because I was attuned to the frequencies by virtue of my psychic work. It was a sound that I will never forget until my dying day.

Finally, I experienced a classic example of a purely *emotional* response to a place and its former use in the Mittersill Castle rooted deep in the mountains, high above the town of Mittersill in the Pinzgau area of Austria.

The castle was constructed in the twelfth century, and it was strategically placed there to control and tax merchant traffic passing through the Thurn Pass, one of the few routes from Italy. It had a chequered history and was used as a regional court for over six hundred years, including persecutions and witch hunts from the sixteenth to the eighteenth century.

At one corner of the castle was the Witches Tower, under which was a terrible place. Beneath the tower was a round cell of about fifteen feet wide, that rose vertically for over twenty feet before it constricted into a round hole in the ceiling that was approximately three feet wide. It resembled a very large stone wine bottle, but instead of a stopper, it had a hinged metal grill, which provided the only light.

For many hundreds of years, it was used as a prison for those considered to be witches. It was believed that these individuals used their evil powers to create natural disasters. When apprehended, the poor unfortunates were thrown through the open grill in the ceiling to fall twenty feet onto the solid stone floor below. Their legs broke, and they were left to die in agony amongst the decaying cadavers.

If the suspected witches were afforded the luxury of a trial, which was seldom, they were suspended from the ceiling in a cage until the trial took place. People of the time believed that if the accused could stand on the ground, they could draw power and float up to an altitude where they could not be dealt with. It appears ridiculous in this day and age, but in those dark, superstitious times, it was a reality.

I entered the dark cell, and my emotions were instantly overcome by the powerful energies that had been absorbed by the walls. The pain and despair hung in the air, and I was able to remain for only a short while. This experience affected me deeply and remains with me always.

Glossary

I hope that this brief glossary will be useful to clarify any of the lesser known descriptions that I have used in this book.

Ghosts
Cogent personalities who:
- may not know that they are dead,
- are linked to the place where they have been troubled or wronged or have a strong emotional attachment to,
- have unfinished business which they perceive they have to deal with.
- are frightened to proceed on their way,
- or simply want to make contact with someone in their former world.

Psychic
Being psychic means that you are, or you are capable of, tuning in to the subtle, unseen realm by using that sixth sense that picks up thoughts, feelings, and atmospheres from outside oneself. This can be on a rational or irrational, conscious or unconscious level of the psyche.

Thought Forms
Entities brought into existence by the power of thought. When someone or a group of people, alive or dead, focus on an idea or fear, it can produce a thought form. The thought form could be God, a demonic being, or simply an energy object. It exists only in the lower astral plane but is capable of manifesting in the earth plane when circumstances allow.

Elementals
Inhabitants of the lower astral plane. Often mischievous and untrustworthy. Created by focussed thoughts or desires.

Poltergeists
Non-cogent entity manifestations, often created by teenage children going through puberty or by emotionally charged individuals. Generally havoc-creating energies with physical phenomena often being experienced.

Portals
Links between planes of existence that allow the movement of entities between the physical and lower astral planes. They are three-dimensional and can occur anywhere and at any time but often appear, from personal experience, on energy node points.

Embedded Memories (Psychic Residues)
The energy residue left behind at a location. Residues can arise from old emotions, thoughts, behaviours, and experiences and from people who have lived or died somewhere.

Non-Cogent Entities
Often confused with entities, but invariably a psychic residue or imprint embedded in the place of manifestation as a result of a traumatic event or a strong emotional link. Cannot be communicated with, as no cogent personality exists. May occur randomly, as specific energies become available, or may be dependent on a given date.

Primordial Fear
Fear is the primordial emotion, the survival response upon which we and our forebears have always relied. It is heightened by darkness and the unknown.

Higher Self
The part of your consciousness that is eternal, divine, and all-seeing. Your higher self functions beyond the confines of the earth plane and can therefore guide and guard you from a place of wisdom.

Aura
The subtle energy field that surrounds all physical bodies—a multi-layered, perceivable personal energy field. A leaky aura means that there is a hole or tear in the field that surrounds the body, allowing energy or outside influences to pass into or be drawn out of a person's psychic space without being obvious.

Astral Plane
The often unseen plane closest in vibrational frequency to our world (the rate of vibration distinguishes between the different levels). This is the plane that most souls travel to immediately after death and from whence comes most communication we receive. Ignorance, lack of awareness that death has occurred, and the pull of grieving relatives will often trap souls in this plane.

Electromagnetic Stress
The frequency created by the plethora of man-made energies that constantly bombard us in our modern world. A potent mix of electrical, magnetic, microwave, and radio frequencies are implicated in many forms of cancer, myalgic encephalomyelitis, and other diseases. This has a disastrous effect on our subtle bodies and immune systems, and it removes our ability to fight off many diseases and ailments.

Geopathic Stress
Radiations from the earth (also with a lunar content) that give an unfavourable reaction to the human biological system and can close down or otherwise affect the immune system. Often attracts ghosts when negative, especially at node points.

Gatekeeper (Doorkeeper)
A guardian angel or spirit who guards the psychic gateways (portals) that link us to the unseen world.

Space Smudging
The use of smoke to cleanse space. Based on an age-old Native American tradition, using a combination of sacred herbs such as cedar, sweet grass, copal, or lavender burnt to produce a cleansing smoke.

Psychic Attachment
A personality or being deceased or alive, influencing someone by auric attachment, which influences him or her adversely. Psychic attachment can also occur in relation to objects. Psychic penetration can occur when the body's aura is compromised, allowing energy, thoughts, and emotions to pass through.

Quintessences
Essences created to bring the energy of colour rays into the auric sphere. Raises the potential for access to the universal mind and higher energies. Often used for protection.

Pomanders
These come in many types and are a catalyst of herbs, plants, and colours. Each essence contains specific vibration and wavelength values that can be used for many different purposes. For example, red pomander affords protection for those working with earth energies and sacred sites. Deep-red pomander is a powerful grounding agent and meditation enhancer.

Chakras
Energy centres that link the personal energy field with the physical body.

Demonic Beings
Elemental spirits with evil intent, often inhabiting the lower astral plane (see thought forms).

Black Streams
A term used by dowsers to denote an underground stream that is not potable and that gives off energies that are detrimental to one's health. Generally meanders as a river or underground water course.

Vortices
The form that energy can take, normally at a crossing point of energy lines (node point). Can ascend or descend vertically, and changes in polarity from positive to negative can occur.

Etheric Body
The subtle body that forms a vehicle for the soul to exist independently of the physical body. Contains spiritual, mental, and emotional components.

Egg Breath . . .
A form of positive visualisation technique designed to encase the practitioner in an egg shaped field, in various colours, as deemed necessary, as a protection from outside influences

Undercroft . . .
In architecture an undercroft is a subterranean room of any kind but especially one under a church, or one used as a chapel or for any sacred purpose.

Other books of the author in AuthorHouse:

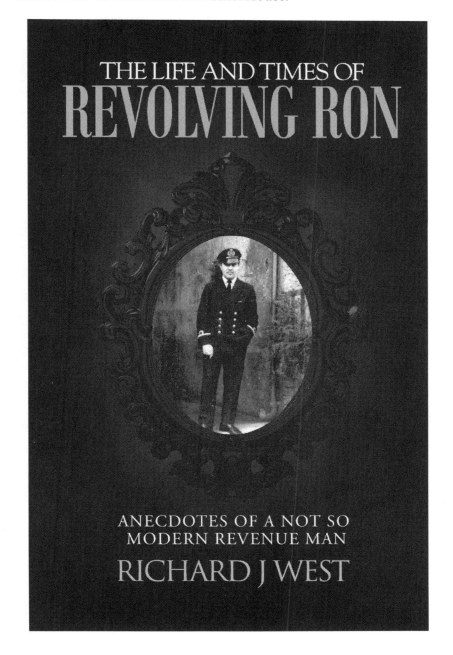

About the Author

Richard began his working life as an HM customs officer, where he was awarded two Queen's Commendations for outstanding success in the line of duty. Since then he has run his own building and construction companies for 35 years, not only giving him an extensive grounding and practical knowledge of the trade—collecting qualifications in electrical engineering and plumbing along the way—but also an understanding of the demands and stresses of the business environment. In 1996 he founded The Priory, a complementary therapy centre.

After completing five years of study both in the Reiki discipline—he is a Usui Reiki Master and teacher—and also with personal mentors, Richard became a Healer Member of the National Federation of

Spiritual Healers. Richard is also a member of the Spirit Release Foundation.

He was a serving member of the Council of the British Society of Dowsers and on the Professional Register since1995. Richard has worked for many years as a successful geopathic stress consultant, water dowser, and ghost buster both in the UK, USA and in Europe.

Made in the USA
Las Vegas, NV
05 November 2023

80286129R00074